COMPETITION IN EDUCATION

A CASE STUDY OF INTERDISTRICT CHOICE

COMPETITION IN EDUCATION

A CASE STUDY OF INTERDISTRICT CHOICE

David J. Armor

and

Brett M. Peiser

Pioneer Institute
Boston, Massachusetts

© 1997 Pioneer Institute for Public Policy Research

Pioneer Institute is an independent, nonprofit research organization funded by individuals, corporations, and foundations. Pioneer Papers and Dialogues are published for educational purposes, to assist policymakers and to broaden public understanding for critical social and economic issues. Views expressed in the Institute's publications are those of the authors and not necessarily those of the Pioneer staff, advisors, or directors, nor should they be construed as an attempt to influence any election or legislative action.

Cover Art: Ralph Buglass, Winchester, Massachusetts
Printing: Pitney Bowes, Stamford, Connecticut
Desktop Publishing: WordSmith, Rockland, Massachusetts

Library of Congress Cataloging-in-Publication Data

Armor, David J.
    Competition in education : a case study of interdistrict choice / David J. Armor and Brett M. Peiser.
      p. cm. -- (Pioneer paper : no. 12)
   Includes bibliographical references and index.
   ISBN 0-929930-17-7
    1. School choice--Massachusetts--Case studies. 2. School enrollment--Massachusetts--Case studies. 3. School districts--Massachusetts--Finance--Case studies. I. Peiser, Brett M., 1968- II. Title. III. Series: Pioneer paper ; no. 12.
LB1027.9.A76 1997
379.1'11--dc21   97-11432
                                                                                       CIP

Pioneer Institute for Public Policy Research

Pioneer Institute is a public policy research organization that specializes in the support, distribution, and promotion of scholarly research on Massachusetts public policy issues. Its main program—the Pioneer Paper series—consists of research projects commissioned from area scholars. The Institute publishes these papers and communicates the research results to decision makers in government and opinion leaders in business, academia, and the media. Pioneer Institute is supported by corporate, foundation, and individual contributions and qualifies under IRS rules for 501 (c)(3) tax-exempt status.

Board of Directors

Lovett C. Peters, *Founding Chairman*
Colby Hewitt, Jr., *Chairman*
John W. Rowe, *Vice Chairman*
Charles D. Baker, Sr.
James F. Carlin
Paul W. Cronin
William S. Edgerly
David C. Evans

Cindy Johnson
Thomas P. McDermott
Joseph C. McNay
Peter Nessen
Diana Spencer
Raymond Shamie
Thornton Stearns
Virginia Straus

Pioneer Staff

James A. Peyser, *Executive Director*
Morris Gray, *Treasurer*
Linda Brown
Robert S. Chatfield
Charles D. Chieppo

Patricia A. Maddox
Heather Morton
Gabriela Mrad
Kit J. Nichols

Board of Academic Advisors

Randy E. Barnett
Brigitte Berger
Jeffrey S. Flier
Nathan Glazer
Harvey C. Mansfield, Jr.

Jeffrey A. Miron
Simon Rottenberg
Richard Schmalensee
Abigail Thernstrom

Pioneer Institute recognizes the generous support of its members. It is only with your support—financial and otherwise—that Pioneer can continue to publish studies and sponsor forums.

TABLE OF CONTENTS

Foreword ix

Acknowledgments xii

Chapter One: Introduction and Summary 1

Chapter Two: Research on School Choice 13

Chapter Three: Study Background and Design 33

Chapter Four: Social, Racial, and Financial Impacts of Choice 47

Chapter Five: Does Market Competition Improve Schools? 77

Chapter Six: Views and Attitudes About Choice 111

Chapter Seven: Conclusions and Policy Recommendations 141

Appendix A 151

Appendix B 155

Index 169

About the Authors

FOREWORD

The argument over school choice has been one of the liveliest education policy debates of recent years. Proponents sometimes argue that choice will cure all that ails schooling in America. Opponents often contend that it will wreck education in particular and society in general. The fact is that school choice, by itself, is no panacea. (Neither is it a hostile act!) Rather, it is one of many reforms necessary to break out of the mediocrity that has characterized American education in recent decades. I often think of choice as the key lubricant of any serious education reform strategy.

During the 1980s, parental choice within public education emerged as a significant reform idea. By 1990, nine states had enacted laws providing, in effect, that children could attend public school anywhere in the state. (More have since jumped on this bandwagon.) Even in its limited, public-school-only version, widening acceptance of choice was a momentous development. It signaled that the nation is beginning to slough off the old assumptions that schools should be identical, that children are interchangeable, that parents can be ignored, and that students can be moved around and assigned to schools like pawns on the chessboards of distant policymakers.

Families must be able to select their schools—and to leave them if dissatisfied or if a better option arises. Solid information about all the schooling options available to families is obviously vital for successful decisionmaking by parents and children. On the supply side, too, the array of schools from which they may choose should be as diverse as possible. That's why I'm also bullish on charter schools, on public schools managed under contract to private firms, and on scholarship (or voucher) programs such as those now funded by the state in Milwaukee and Cleveland and by private philanthropies in dozens of other communities.

The authors of *Competition in Education: A Case Study of Interdistrict Choice* build on the central argument made by John Chubb and Terry Moe (and earlier by Milton Friedman and others), that the incentives and dynamics of the marketplace must be brought to bear if we are to effect real change in our education system. Introducing the elements of a competitive environment into troubled school systems can only improve the quality of the services offered to families in Massachusetts and elsewhere.

David Armor and Brett Peiser cogently present their hypothesis and describe the results that should be expected if their proposition is true—and those that would indicate it is not. They go on to show that, given a chance (and enough information) to choose, most families make decisions on the basis of the quality of academic programs and school standards. Moreover, most families who choose schools are extremely satisfied with their selections.

The authors found that school districts losing significant numbers of students as a result of interdistrict choice commonly responded by making programmatic changes designed to make their schools more attractive to their "customers," just as the theory of competition says they would and should do. Districts feeling less of an enrollment (or budgetary) jolt from student choice had less incentive to strengthen their educational offerings. The authors rightly conclude that competition leads districts to reconsider the quality of their educational services and to make purposeful efforts to retain enrollment. Indeed, schools operating under the pressure of competition appear more apt to produce the kind of services that satisfy parents and children.

The originality of this study lies in the fact that Armor and Peiser have focused on real data—something absent from many heated, but abstract, debates over educational choice. They deserve praise for bringing facts into this discussion and for fairly stating the arguments of both sides. Their analysis and the data they present will no doubt influence the debate at the national level. Furthermore, they offer invaluable information to Massachusetts voters and policymakers who are weighing the success of the Commonwealth's interdistrict choice program and considering ways to improve it.

Chester E. Finn, Jr.
Washington, D.C.
March 1997

Chester E. Finn, Jr., is the John M. Olin Fellow at the Hudson Institute and former Assistant U.S. Secretary of Education for Research and Improvement.

ACKNOWLEDGMENTS

The authors gratefully acknowledge the many individuals and organizations that made important contributions to this study. First and foremost are the staff of the Pioneer Institute: Jim Peyser, who proposed this project and offered conceptual assistance throughout; Gabriela Mrad, who provided valuable assistance throughout the project—from funding to design and editing; Kim Kosman, who coded and analyzed the school staff interviews; and Kathryn Ciffolillo, who rendered extensive editorial services. We would also like to thank those individuals and foundations who provided Pioneer with funding for this project.

The study would not have been possible without the willingness of administrators and school committee members in our 19 case study school districts to participate in lengthy personal interviews. Our thanks also extend to the many choice families who participated in the parent and student surveys, and to Ron Smith and his staff at AMRIGON who conducted the parent interviews.

Finally, we greatly appreciate the assistance of our reviewers, who offered many helpful suggestions and criticisms of earlier drafts: Mike Ronan, Bruce Fuller, Joe Nathan, Scott Hamilton, Bryan Hassel, Paul Peterson, and Paul Hill. While we acknowledge the contributions of others, we take full responsibility for the final report.

CHAPTER ONE

INTRODUCTION AND SUMMARY

In the spring of 1991, Massachusetts adopted a comprehensive interdistrict school choice law, joining a growing number of states that have adopted some type of open enrollment policy on a statewide basis. The Massachusetts program began small but grew steadily. Only about 1,000 students changed school districts during the 1991–92 school year. By the 1995–96 school year, nearly 6,800 students had opted to attend school in another district, and about two-thirds of Massachusetts school districts were being affected in some way, by sending (losing) students, receiving (gaining) students, or both. This places Massachusetts among the states with the largest interdistrict choice populations.

THE DEBATE OVER SCHOOL CHOICE

School choice has long been the subject of intense debate, and the Massachusetts version is no exception. Choice proponents stress the academic benefits for choice students who are stuck in mediocre school systems, or who might benefit from particular programs not available in their home systems. Further, proponents often invoke the "market competition" thesis, arguing that expanded school choice will actually improve education by forcing weak school systems to upgrade their academic programs in order to attract and retain good students. Finally, proponents assert that affluent families already have school choice because they can afford to move to another community or pay for private schools, so that low-income families who cannot now afford to move or to use private schools may well be the greatest beneficiaries of choice. This argument assumes, of course, that disadvantaged families are aware of and will use the choice options.

Critics of school choice usually advance an "elitist" argument, that choice will mainly benefit affluent or at least middle-class families who have the least need for enhanced school quality. They argue that education is harmed because advantaged students will leave poorer, weaker school districts in search of stronger programs in more affluent communities, leaving behind low-income students in increasingly disadvantaged school systems. They also argue that low-income families are less likely to be informed about the choice program than middle-class families, thereby making lower participation inevitable. The result, they maintain, is that weak schools become weaker and strong schools become stronger.

SCHOOL CHOICE IN MASSACHUSETTS

Massachusetts interdistrict choice was signed into law by Governor William F. Weld in March 1991 as part of a fiscal recovery act. The Education Reform Act of 1993 required that districts vote yearly on whether to accept choice students; districts cannot prevent transfers out. If a district chooses to become a receiving district, it cannot apply any selection criteria to individual students, and the number of transfers in is limited only by school capacity. The total number of students who can participate is capped at 2 percent of the state's total public school enrollment.

Two unique aspects of the Massachusetts program drew additional fire from critics. First, unlike most statewide open enrollment programs, Massachusetts has no restrictions whatsoever regarding racial impacts. That is, white students can transfer from districts with high minority populations to those with fewer minority students, and minority students can move in the opposite direction, even if the losses or gains have an adverse impact on a school desegregation plan.

Second, rather than having state funds follow the transferring student, the district sending the student has to pay full tuition costs—including those funded with local property taxes—out of its own state aid. One reason for this payment feature has to do with replicating market conditions, where competition for students is assumed to force school districts to either improve their programs or lose income. If there is no financial penalty for a school district that loses more students than it gains, clearly there is less incentive for that district to improve its programs and recover its losses.

The state's policy was not well received by those districts that lost a significant number of students in the early years of the program, many of which had relatively high levels of poor and minority students. In 1993, the state legislature did make a number of changes to the choice program, mostly in the area of financing. The most important changes were to place a limit of $5,000 or 75 percent of per pupil expenditure on the tuition paid to receiving districts for each transferring student, and to provide for at least partial reimbursement of tuition payments made by sending districts. As a result of these changes and expansions in state funding for education provided for in the Reform Act, some of the harsher criticisms of the choice policy have abated.

THE STUDY

It is precisely its unique program features that make the Massachusetts choice law attractive for study. To our knowledge, Massachusetts is the only state with a significant minority population that does not include racial restrictions in its interdistrict choice policy. One of our major research questions is whether the Massachusetts choice program has had adverse effects on racial balance, particularly for districts with higher minority enrollments. Closely related to this question is the representativeness of choice students, and whether choice is being utilized by all types of students. In view of the tuition payment policies, we also want to inquire about the financial impacts of choice, particularly its effects on low-wealth sending districts with high minority enrollments.

The tuition payment policy, while criticized by many as unfair or punitive to sending districts, also makes the Massachusetts program especially attractive for testing the market competition thesis. If the competition theory is correct, we would expect the most affected sending districts to introduce programmatic changes in order to win back lost students or attract new ones. This thesis, sometimes expressed as "no pain, no gain," can only be tested if there are significant financial rewards and penalties for net receiving and sending school districts, which is a major feature of the Massachusetts policy. Accordingly, a second major research question addressed by this study is the validity of the market competition thesis as applied to public school choice.

Finally, we must consider the role of the choice population itself. The market competition thesis depends on the perceived and actual costs and benefits of choice to the consumer, in this case students and their families. In order for a penalty and reward system to work, a district that is losing more students than it gains must be able to address the problem causing the losses. If the reasons students leave a district are primarily academic and programmatic in nature, then the district can presumably make the necessary changes to improve its competitive position. If the reasons for choice losses are primarily related to racial or social prejudices, as some critics argue, then most net sending districts would not be able to reverse the losses because they cannot change their demographic makeup. Accordingly, the third major research question in this study concerns the role and view of families who have chosen to leave their home districts, and particularly the reasons parents and students give for changing school districts. The views of school district staff on the question of motivation are also considered.

Ideally, a choice policy should also be judged by whether it improves academic outcomes for the choice population. Since the resources available for this study did not permit a comprehensive assessment of academic outcomes, the major thrust of this study is the structural and systemic impacts of choice.

This study focuses primarily on interdistrict public school choice rather than two other school choice options in Massachusetts, charter schools and the METCO voluntary desegregation program. The charter school option was just getting started when this study began, while the METCO program has a very different purpose and structure. We will include these two programs when evaluating racial representation, however, because they are the only options available to Boston minority students, given that most Boston suburbs do not accept interdistrict choice students.

Before addressing our specific research questions, chapter 2 will provide a context for this study by reviewing literature and research in the general area of school choice. Chapter 3 will review the history of the Massachusetts choice law, present some basic data on choice schools and enrollment, and lay out our study design. The first cluster of research questions will be taken up in chapter 4, which will examine the social, racial, and financial impacts of choice using statewide data.

Chapter 5 will then address the market competition thesis, relying primarily on case studies of 20 school districts and state data. For the case studies we selected a non-random sample of 10 pairs of school districts, one being a net receiving district with more than 100 transfers in and one being a net sending district with the largest number of transfers to that receiver (all but one sender also had 100 or more transfers out). This sample represents more than half of the largest senders and receivers in the state.

Chapter 6 presents our findings on the attitudes of Massachusetts parents, students, and residents towards school choice, with special emphasis on the reasons for changing school districts. These data are drawn from three surveys, two of which were designed specifically for this study. Chapter 7 presents a general discussion of our findings along with some policy recommendations based on those findings.

CONCLUSIONS

1. We find no significant effects on racial balance or on the financial health of sending districts with high minority and poverty concentrations. The reason for this finding is that the districts with the highest concentrations of minority and low-income students also have large total enrollments. When the choice losses are expressed as percentages, the impact on racial composition in these districts is less than 1 percentage point and the impact on total expenditures is between .5 and 1.5 percent. In fact, the effect of choice actually raises the percent minority of net receiving districts to a somewhat greater degree than it lowers the percent minority in sending districts, albeit the effects are small.

   We found that receiving districts tend to be more affluent and less minority than sending districts *on average,* and also that interdistrict choice students tend to be more affluent, more academically skilled, and less minority than the *average* sending school population. On the other hand, considerable choice is occurring among districts that are predominantly white, where race cannot be an issue, and there are a significant number of instances among the largest net sending districts in which choice students are actually academically less skilled than their respective resident populations. If we consider all net senders together, the differences in social and academic characteristics between senders and receivers are not as large as critics have argued.

If we look only at the composition of the interdistrict choice population, we find minorities are underrepresented compared to the state as a whole, but this difference diminishes if Boston is excluded. However, if we combine enrollment in all Massachusetts choice programs, including METCO and charter schools, we find good racial and ethnic representation. In fact, African-American students are actually overrepresented in choice programs in comparison to the total state population.

2. We conclude that the market competition thesis is valid for the Massachusetts interdistrict choice program. We found that six of the nine net sending districts for which we have data responded in ways consistent with the market thesis. Those sending districts most severely affected by enrollment losses responded by improving their policies and programs in order to win back students or attract new ones. Another group of sending districts— which experienced no significant negative effects on programs, staffing, or resources—did not respond to choice losses. Most important, those districts that made programmatic changes slowed or reversed their choice losses, while those that did not continued to lose students at the same rate.

Although the interdistrict choice law has been criticized for its adverse financial effects on low-wealth districts, we find that the state foundation aid program has ameliorated the adverse

financial effects of choice, reducing the incentive for some of these districts to examine and improve their academic programs.
3. With regard to the role and attitudes of choice families and citizens, we find that the motivations of parents and students for changing schools are consistent with the market thesis and contradict critics who claim that parents leave higher minority or low-wealth districts for racial or social reasons. The vast majority of choice parents and students, staff at receiving districts, and even staff at some sending districts cite academic and programmatic features as the main reasons for choosing a school district. The predominant reason is academic standards, which families perceive to be higher in their schools of choice than in their home districts.

Finally, all the survey and interview data in this study show substantial support for expanded school choice in general and interdistrict public school choice in particular. We find that even a majority of school administrators from net sending districts support interdistrict choice, albeit with some modifications, with the strongest support coming from the districts initially most affected—since choice ultimately spurred them to revitalize their academic programs.

We also find that support for interdistrict choice is stronger among African-American and Hispanic residents than among white residents. When this fact is coupled with the high rate of participation in the METCO program, we conclude that the underrepresentation of minority families in the current interdistrict choice program is due to some combination of lack of access, low awareness about choice options, and perceived or actual lack of transportation assistance.

Increased transportation subsidy was the most frequent recommendation of choice families, with mandatory participation for all districts second. The most frequent recommendation for changes by school staff, receiver and sender alike, was to shift the burden of financial payments from the sending districts to the state.

RECOMMENDATIONS

The study recommends that the Massachusetts interdistrict choice program be continued, albeit with some modifications. The evidence in its favor includes the facts that many thousands of families are using it, they are very happy with it, and it has led to significant program improvements in some of the most impacted sending districts. It is also supported by a majority of school staff in our case study districts.

Our recommendations deal mainly with improving minority and low-income representation—which we believe is not consistent with their potential for participation—and adjusting the tuition payment formulas.

1. AWARENESS ASSESSMENT

The state should conduct a survey to assess the interest in and awareness of interdistrict choice options among public school parents, especially minority and low-income families. The survey should also test awareness and adequacy of current transportation subsidies for low-income families.

2. TRANSPORTATION

Given the frequency of transportation complaints from choice families and school staff, the state should evaluate the adequacy of the present transportation assistance, particularly with regard to its adequacy for low-income families. The evaluation should include funding levels, timeliness and means of reimbursement, and any other regulations that may impede the efficient delivery of transportation assistance.

3. ADVERTISING

In order to improve awareness of choice options, all school districts should be required to inform any adjacent (or nearby) districts of the number of seats available for choice transfers, as well as advertise in local newspapers. All districts should be required to inform their own resident students of which adjacent (or nearby) school districts have seats available for choice transfers, as well as the availability of transportation.

4. ACCESS

To improve accessibility of interdistrict choice for low-income and minority parents, and to maximize the benefits of choice for all families and school systems in the state, all school districts should be required to accept choice students if there is space available. School boards would retain control over the determination of physical capacity, although capacity should not be manipulated to keep out students from other districts. We note that mandatory district participation in no way impairs local control over curriculum, academic standards, and staffing decisions.

5. TUITION PAYMENTS

All reimbursement for tuition losses should be phased out within a year or two after making choice mandatory for all districts. Since foundation aid is already increasing the funding of low-wealth school districts to put them on a par with all districts, there should be less need to offer special reimbursements for below-foundation districts as foundation goals are realized over the next several years. There need to be clear financial rewards and penalties for gaining or losing market share, and the reimbursement system tends to work against market forces.

A study of marginal, variable, and fixed costs would be in order for Massachusetts schools. Based on such as study, the state could develop a general formula for tuition payments based on the actual marginal costs of educating additional (or fewer) students, plus some reward for attracting students. Such a formula might help dispel views that choice unfairly penalizes net sending districts or improperly rewards net receiving districts.

CHAPTER TWO

RESEARCH ON SCHOOL CHOICE

This chapter reviews recent writings and research on school choice, taking a broad perspective that includes choice policies such as voucher plans and charter schools. This review will also make clear how this study differs from other studies or evaluations of choice.

Though past evaluation studies have defined school choice in several different ways, most school choice policies can be categorized somewhere along the continuum from intradistrict public school choice to private school voucher plans. We can identify four major types of choice plans:

- Intradistrict choice programs allow parents and students to select any public school within their home district and are often designed to meet court-ordered racial balance requirements (e.g., controlled choice).

- Interdistrict choice programs allow students to attend public schools outside their home district and are limited by space constraints and students' transportation needs; restrictions on racial impact often exist.

- Charter schools are publicly financed schools run by teachers, parents, and local community members under a charter granted by the state.

- Voucher plans give parents tuition vouchers redeemable at private schools or at private and public schools.

What unites these plans is that they break the link between residence and schooling by offering parents and children the opportunity to choose schools outside their home district. Our analysis will focus only on the latter three choice forms, since intradistrict "controlled choice" plans such as those in Cambridge, Massachusetts, and in Boston are designed more to promote desegregation than increase choices, and as such they often restrict school choice by mandatory school reassignment. Rather, we are interested in examining those plans that increase school choice and have the potential to "alter the way schools are organized within a state."[1]

THE THEORY

While it has many manifestations, school choice remains an appealingly simple idea: Eliminate student assignment in public schools and allow each school to operate under the same competitive rules as private schools. The students' or parents' freedom to choose which school they will attend will create demand for quality schools. Schools will supply the quality education their customers desire, since the money that keeps them running would follow the students to the schools of their choice.

In the best-known defense of school choice, John E. Chubb and Terry M. Moe suggest three reasons why "markets work to ensure that parents and students play a much more central and influential role in private sector education."[2] The first is that school administrators and faculty "have a strong incentive to please a clientele of parents and students through the decisions they make."[3] It is this consumer-

---

[1] Peter W. Cookson, Jr., *School Choice: The Struggle for the Soul of American Education,* New Haven: Yale University Press, 1994, p. 16.
[2] John E. Chubb and Terry M. Moe, *Politics, Markets, and America's Schools,* Washington, DC: The Brookings Institution, 1990, p. 32.
[3] Chubb and Moe, p. 32.

producer responsiveness that best demonstrates the market match between the wants of parents and students and the kinds of education schools provide. Without family choice, schools have much less immediate incentives to provide an adequate education for students, especially given the high costs of attending a private school and similarly burdensome costs of moving to another district.

The second reason lies with people's economic freedom "to switch from one alternative to another when they think it would be beneficial to do so."[4] When there is a "deterioration in the quality of the product or service provided...some customers stop buying the firm's products or some members leave the organization...[and] as a result, revenues drop, membership declines, and management is impelled to search for ways and means to correct whatever faults have led to exit." If parents and students do not like the services being provided by their current school, they can exit and find another school whose curriculum and environment better suit their needs.[5]

The third and most important reason lies with the process of natural selection:

> Schools that fail to satisfy a sufficiently large clientele will go out of business....Of the schools that survive, those that do a better job of satisfying customers will be more likely to prosper and proliferate. They may be joined or challenged at any time, moreover, by new schools that enter the marketplace to offer similar services in a better way. The dynamics of entry, success, and failure, driven by the requisites of parent-student support, all tend to promote the

---

[4] Chubb and Moe, p. 32.
[5] Albert O. Hirschman, *Exit, Voice, and Loyalty,* Cambridge, Massachusetts: Harvard University Press, 1970, p. 4.

emergence of a population of schools that matches the population of parents and students.[6]

Critics of choice claim that competition is not the solution to the nation's educational woes. Rather than promote fair competition, school choice will promote racial and academic segregation, damage already poorly performing schools by taking away much needed funds, and fall short of providing higher student achievement. Those parents who opt to take advantage of the program will choose their children's schools based on nonacademic criteria such as a school's location or its athletic programs, while those who do not choose will fail to do so because they are unaware of their options or because the state does not provide transportation assistance. Choice policies will leave behind the poor and most difficult to educate, while good students will be creamed into the best schools, exacerbating the already extensive financial and academic disparities between today's schools. Forsaken schools will suffer ever-decreasing levels of student achievement since the most academically talented students will cross over into neighboring districts.

The editors of a recent compendium on school choice have outlined such concerns. First, "increasing educational choice is likely to increase separation of students by race, social class, and cultural background." As they explain,

> If the propensity to choose and children's performance in school are heavily influenced by parents' social class and educational background, then it seems plausible to expect that, other things being equal, increasing parental choice will accelerate both the social stratification of schools and the gap in student performance between schools enrolling high concentrations of poor and working-class students versus

---

[6] Chubb and Moe, p. 33.

those with predominantly white, middle-class students....It seems likely that interdistrict choice plans would provide enhanced opportunities for inner-city parents and students who have a strong achievement orientation but would further isolate parents and students whose expectations are less well formed and whose knowledge of how to take advantage of complex choice options is limited.[7]

Second, "greater choice in public education is unlikely, by itself, to increase either the variety of programs available to students, or the overall performance of schools," since choice programs must operate "in tandem with other educational improvement initiatives to foster" school innovation and student achievement.[8] And third, competitive principles fail to hold because "market theories, for the most part, assume that consumers' preferences can be described and aggregated in relatively simple ways...[but] different groups of educational clients seem not only to have very different predispositions to choose, they also seem to bring very different cultural and social assumptions to the choices they are expected to make."[9]

Unfortunately, the theory regarding the systemic impact of school choice clearly outweighs the empirical evidence. And what empirical evidence is available is subject to interpretation, leading two researchers to comment, the "evidence supports virtually every opinion on school choice."[10] Nevertheless, as more and more states have adopted school choice policies over the past few years, more and

---

[7] Richard F. Elmore and Bruce Fuller, "Empirical Research on Educational Choice: What Are the Implications for Policy-Makers?" in Bruce Fuller, Richard F. Elmore, and Gary Orfield (eds.), *Who Chooses? Who Loses? Culture, Institutions, and the Unequal Effects of School Choice,* New York: Teachers College Press, 1996, p. 191.
[8] Elmore and Fuller, pp. 193–195.
[9] Elmore and Fuller, pp. 197–198.
[10] Kevin B. Smith and Kenneth J. Meier, "School Choice: Panacea or Pandora's Box?" *Phi Delta Kappan* (December 1995): 313.

more evidence of its effects has trickled in for careful study and analysis. Since existing evidence focuses on choice plans that are somewhat different from the Massachusetts model, comparisons and generalizations must be made with a measure of caution. To one degree or another, however, the same market principles—competition for students and the money that follows them—are at work.

In one of the few studies of school choice in Massachusetts, written before the state's interdistrict choice plan began, Abigail Thernstrom offered several recommendations regarding parental choice. She came out against controlled choice because it limits a family's choices by placing too much emphasis on racial balance. She supported an interdistrict public school choice policy, much like the one implemented in 1991, on the grounds that it would enhance the "freedom of families to shape their lives as they see fit." Thernstrom also recommended a privately funded pilot voucher program for disadvantaged students to explore the potential benefits of this "bold and radical" educational concept.[11]

THE EVIDENCE

According to a 1992 report by the Carnegie Foundation, nationwide levels of participation in school choice programs have remained far below program capacity, which may be due to a number of factors. Some of those factors are illustrated in table 2–1, which lists states that have interdistrict open enrollment laws.

First, lack of available space and desegregation plans often constrain student choices. Second, it is possible that "most parents and students are satisfied with their neighborhood schools, or at least

---

[11] Abigail Thernstrom, *School Choice in Massachusetts*, Boston: Pioneer Institute for Public Policy Research, 1991, chapters 2 and 5.

not dissatisfied enough to switch."[12] In a September 1995 Gallup poll, 65 percent of parents gave their oldest child's school a grade of A or B.[13] Third, choice may not have created new education options sufficient to motivate students to cross district lines. Fourth, parent information centers for explaining school choice options exist in only a handful of states. And finally, as table 2-1 indicates, there is a lack of transportation assistance, which may deter families from taking advantage of choice options. Aside from some targeted help offered to low-income families by Iowa, Minnesota, Massachusetts, and Nebraska, "most states leave the transportation up to parents and local school districts."[14]

Table 2-1 shows that various types of racial restrictions also serve to limit participation. Massachusetts is the only state with a significant minority enrollment that has no racial restrictions on its interdistrict choice policy (Idaho, North Dakota, and Utah have very low minority enrollments). For example, school districts in Arkansas, Iowa, Minnesota, Nebraska, Ohio, and Washington may deny district transfers if they would hinder desegregation efforts. In 1993, Iowa's program was revised to include explicit restrictions on transfers and establish strict racial ratios in Des Moines—the state's largest district—after about 125 white students were denied requests to transfer. The school board had denied their applications because over 97 percent of students transferring in the first two years of the program were white.

---

[12] Carnegie Foundation for the Advancement of Teaching, *School Choice, A Special Report,* Princeton, New Jersey, 1992, p. 49.
[13] Stanley M. Elam and Lowell C. Rose, "The 27th Annual Phi Delta Kappa/Gallup Poll of the Public's Attitudes Toward the Public Schools," *Phi Delta Kappan* 77 (September 1995) 1: 41–56.
[14] Carnegie Foundation, p. 49.

Table 2–1
Statewide Open Enrollment Plans

State	Year Program Began	Number of Choice Students[a]	Type of Open Enrollment[b]	Transportation Assistance	Racial Restriction
Arkansas	1990–91	1,912 (1996–97)	Voluntary	None	Yes
California	1989–90	N/A	Voluntary	None	Yes
Idaho	1990–91	3,090 (1995–96)	Voluntary	None	No
Iowa	1990–91	13,959 (1996–97)	Mandatory	For low-income students only	Yes
Massachusetts	1991–92	6,793 (1995–96)	Voluntary	For low-income students only	No
Minnesota	1988–89	18,916 (1995–96)	Mandatory	Expenses tax-deductible	Yes
Nebraska	1990–91	12,119 (1996–97)	Mandatory	For low-income students only	Yes
North Dakota	1993–94	805 (1996–97)	Voluntary	None	No
Ohio	1990–91	16,900 (1996–97)	Voluntary	None	Yes
Utah	1991–92	7,000 (1992–93)	Mandatory	None	No
Washington	1991–92	16,115 (1994–95)	Voluntary	None	Yes

Source: Various state departments of education.

[a] The number of choice students is defined only as those students who change schools as a result of an interdistrict, open enrollment plan. There may be other students in the state who choose their schools according to different parts of a state's overall choice program.

[b] Districts in states with voluntary programs can opt out of the choice program, while those with mandatory programs must receive students, provided space is available.

MILWAUKEE PARENTAL CHOICE PROGRAM

Clearly, when it comes to school choice, details matter. As table 2–2 shows, there are important structural differences between the statewide choice plan in Massachusetts and the Milwaukee Parental Choice Program (MPCP), the first publicly funded private voucher plan in the country. Despite these differences, the same underlying market mechanism is at work: parents and students can choose to attend schools other than those operated by their home districts.

Table 2–2
Comparison of School Choice Programs in
Milwaukee and Massachusetts

MILWAUKEE	MASSACHUSETTS
Publicly funded private voucher program.	Voluntary, statewide open enrollment plan.
Students must come from households with income 1.75 times the poverty line or less.	No income-eligibility requirements.
Students must have been in the Milwaukee Public School District in the prior year.	No prior year school district restrictions.
Eligible schools must be private, nonsectarian schools with no religious affiliation or training.	All public schools are eligible except in districts that have voted not to receive students.
The total number of choice students is limited to 1.5% of the students in the city's public schools—1,450 in 1994–95.	The total number of choice students is limited to 1% (increasing to 2% in 1997) of the students in the state's public schools—8,800 in 1994–95.
Private schools receive the Milwaukee Public School per-pupil, state aid in lieu of tuition—$3,209 in 1994–95.	Participating schools receive 75% of per-pupil costs, or $5,000, whichever is lower.

In the fourth of his yearly evaluations of the MPCP, John F. Witte concluded that "outcomes after four years of the Choice

Program remain mixed." Witte's data show considerable variability in the changes in the reading and math achievement scores not only for choice students but Milwaukee Public School (MPS) students as well. Witte resolves that "there is no systematic evidence that choice students do either better or worse than MPS students."[15] The Carnegie report had also concluded, "whatever else may be said of it, Milwaukee's plan has failed to demonstrate that vouchers can, in and of themselves, spark school improvement....No evidence can be found that the participating students made significant advances or that either the public or private schools have been revitalized by the transfers."[16]

In a critique of the Witte evaluation, Paul E. Peterson concludes that the comparison of choice schools with Milwaukee public schools is "methodologically flawed." Specifically, Peterson objects to the "gross differences between the background characteristics of choice students and those attending Milwaukee public schools."[17] Peterson writes,

> Witte, when comparing choice and public school students, does not take into account parental education, parental occupation, welfare dependency, whether or not the household is headed by one parent or two, a student's native language, and whether a student has severe social problems.[18]

---

[15] John F. Witte, Christopher A. Thorn, Kim M. Pritchard, and Michele Claibourn, "Fourth-Year Report: Milwaukee Parental Choice Program," Department of Political Science and The Robert M. La Follette Institute of Public Affairs, University of Wisconsin-Madison, December 1994, p. v.
[16] Carnegie Foundation, p. 73.
[17] Paul E. Peterson, "A Critique of the Witte Evaluation of Milwaukee's School Choice Program," Center for American Political Studies, Department of Government, Harvard University, Occasional Paper 95–2, February 1995, p. 14.
[18] Paul E. Peterson and Chad Noyes, "Under Extreme Duress, School Choice Success," Program in Education Policy and Governance, Occasional Paper 96–1, February 1996, p. 33.

Every important study of student achievement has found that family background characteristics are among the most important determinants of student achievement. Any measure of school effects must either take these characteristics into account or hopelessly mislead readers.[19]

Furthermore, Peterson adds, "before entering choice schools, students had lower test scores and greater problems with public school than those who remained in public school."[20]

Peterson and several other researchers have recently found that Milwaukee choice students who attend private schools post higher test scores in reading and math, after three and four years, than their public school counterparts. This is despite the fact that Catholic schools cannot participate in the MPCP, that the private schools that do participate work with less money per student than the Milwaukee public schools, and that the plan has been operating for only four years.

By all accounts, the plan has increased parents' satisfaction with their children's schools. Applications to and participation in the program have grown steadily, from 577 applications in 1990–91 to 1,046 in 1994–95, and from 345 enrollees in the first year to 830 four years later. While there were seven schools participating in the program initially, there are now 12. Overall attrition from the program—the percentage of students who did not graduate and could have returned to school the following year—has declined from 46 percent in 1990–91 to 27 percent in 1993–94, rates lower than those for Milwaukee's low-income public school students. Satisfaction ratings have been 10 to 14 percentage points higher among parents of choice school students than comparable parents in the city's public

---

[19] Peterson, p. 21.
[20] Peterson and Noyes, p. 33.

schools.[21] And finally, for low-income students who comprise over 60 percent of the program, the vouchers have given them greater choice in making their schooling decisions.

EDUCATIONAL CHOICE CHARITABLE TRUST

Private voucher models, in which mostly low-income students are awarded privately funded scholarships to enable them to leave public schools for private education, offer another window on the systemic impact of school choice. The Educational CHOICE Charitable Trust of Indianapolis was the first privately funded voucher program in the country; other such programs now exist in Albany, Atlanta, Little Rock, Milwaukee, and San Antonio. Begun in 1991, the CHOICE program is underwritten by the Golden Rule Insurance Company and offers scholarships of up to $800 a year to help lower income, inner-city families send their children to private schools.

According to a recently released study by the Hudson Institute, "CHOICE students who move from public to private schools see their academic achievement rise slightly, most notably in the middle-school years."[22] The Institute found that among 8th graders who took the reading portion of the state's skills test, CHOICE students in private schools scored nearly 13 points above the Indianapolis Public Schools (IPS) average. Among 6th graders, the same comparison showed a private school advantage of nearly five points.

The authors themselves caution that the scores of the private school students were taken from seven inner-city Catholic schools, not from all of the 67 private schools participating in the scholarship program. Only those seven schools administered the same test at the

---

[21] Statistics culled from Witte et al. and Peterson reports.
[22] David J. Weinschrott and Sally J. Kilgore, "Educational CHOICE Charitable Trust: An Experiment in School Choice," Hudson Briefing Paper, Number 189, Hudson Institute, 1996.

same time as IPS. Furthermore, the results of the study were based on surveys returned by just 40 to 50 percent of CHOICE parents. And as critics of the Indianapolis plan have been quick to point out, the results are unsurprising since such schools are controlled environments and selectively choose their student population.

MINNESOTA OPEN ENROLLMENT PLAN

It is no coincidence that the school choice plan that most closely resembles that of Massachusetts is the system currently in place in Minnesota. Like Massachusetts, Minnesota has a large number of small school districts and a strong tradition of local control of education. In 1988, the Minnesota state legislature established a voluntary system of statewide, intra- and interdistrict open enrollment, in which K–12 students could attend schools outside the districts in which they live. In 1990, the program became mandatory for all districts, meaning that students' resident districts must allow them to leave, and districts must accept all comers provided there is available space.

Minnesota offers a broad array of mechanisms through which elementary and secondary school students in the state may attend school somewhere other than in the district in which they reside. Among them are the following:

- The Open Enrollment Option allows students in grades K–12 to apply to enroll in schools located outside of their resident district.

- The Postsecondary Enrollment Option enables academically eligible juniors and seniors in high school to enroll in college courses prior to graduation from high school.

- The High School Graduation Incentive Program (HSGIP) provides students at risk of dropping out of high school with opportunities to complete the necessary course work for graduation.

- Area Learning Centers are designed as a specific choice for HSGIP youth and provide individualized programs that focus on academics and workforce preparation.

- Public and Private Alternative Programs are second-chance programs for at-risk students and offer a small school atmosphere and a personalized approach to education.[23]

Overall, 14 percent of students in Minnesota actively chose the school they were attending in 1992–93, and participation has increased every year since the program's inception.[24] Use of the school choice options by minority students is also on the rise, having increased by 400 students since 1990–91. Available data for six of the largest programs indicate that, statewide, minority students and their families choose the school they will attend at the same rate as white students and families.[25]

According to a joint federal-state study of the state's open enrollment program, parents listed academic reputation as the single most important reason for transferring their children, followed by educational services, proximity to home, and learning environment.[26] This finding runs contrary to the oft-cited notion that families make their transfer decisions based on nonacademic criteria, and supports other studies, such as those in Arizona and Indianapolis, which found

---

[23] Kelly Colopy and Hope C. Tarr, *Minnesota's Public School Choice Options,* Washington, DC: Policy Studies Associates, Inc., 1994, pp. 1–2.
[24] Joe Nathan and James Ysseldyke, "What Minnesota Has Learned About School Choice," *Phi Delta Kappan,* Vol. 75, No. 9 (May 1994): 683.
[25] Colopy and Tarr, p. 6.
[26] Michael C. Rubenstein, Rosalind Hammar, and Nancy J. Edelman, *Minnesota's Open Enrollment Option,* Washington, DC: Policy Studies Associates, Inc., 1994.

that these decisions are made because of "academic quality" or "the educational quality of the new school."[27]

Richard Fossey found similar results in a comparison of Massachusetts sending and receiving districts during the first two years of the interdistrict choice program. While his study did attempt to measure the social and financial impact of school choice in the state, he was limited by a lack of data on choice student socioeconomic status. The study did reveal that in districts in which 20 or more school choice students transferred,

> Families enrolled their children in districts that had higher median family incomes and better educated adult populations than their home communities. They also went to districts that had better standardized test scores at the high school level, lower out-of-school suspension rates, lower dropout rates, and higher per-pupil funding....These early indications strongly suggest that families are not making decisions to change districts for reasons of mere convenience. On the contrary, families seemed to be making rational decisions when transferring their children out of their home communities, choosing districts with higher indicators of student performance and higher socioeconomic status than the districts they left.[28]

This runs counter to earlier studies such as the 1992 Carnegie Report, which concluded, after reviewing other interdistrict plans, that choice and competition would not prompt academic achievement because "when parents do select another school, academic concerns often are not central to the decision."[29] In a 1994 study of Minnesota's

---

[27] Weinschrott and Kilgore, p. 8; Tara Ellman, "Arizona School Choice Trust: Survey of Participating Families," Arizona Issue Analysis #138, Phoenix, Arizona: Goldwater Institute, January 1996, p. 11.
[28] Richard Fossey, "Open Enrollment in Massachusetts: Why Families Choose," *Educational Evaluation and Policy Analysis,* Vol. 16, No. 3 (Fall 1994): 330–331.
[29] Carnegie Foundation, p. 13.

choice program, researchers found that "the claim that Open Enrollment stimulates schools and school districts to change or improve their programming to meet the demands of consumers remains in question." They point to some evidence that Open Enrollment has had "an impact on school programs, particularly in districts that have lost significant numbers or proportions of students through Open Enrollment." For example, in response to losing students, several districts have reported making special transportation arrangements, expanding course offerings, making physical plant improvements, and increasing extracurricular offerings.[30]

However, "other evidence suggests that Open Enrollment may have little, if any, effect on school change." Open Enrollment has had little overall effect on district finances, and "there appears to be little effect on many educational outcomes, except in a very limited number of districts....While administrators reported changes in several educational indicators over the last five years, [they] pointed to factors other than Open Enrollment as causing change in these indicators."[31]

Despite disagreement over whether Minnesota's programs have sparked programmatic changes, the various choice programs have been very popular with state residents. A recent University of Minnesota-Twin Cities report found that parents express higher than average rates of satisfaction with the state's charter schools. Moreover, the schools enjoy lower than average rates of suspension, and enroll greater concentrations of nonwhite, disabled, poor, and limited English proficient students than other public schools in their

---

[30] Janie E. Funkhouser and Kelly Colopy, *Minnesota's Open Enrollment Option: Impacts on School Districts,* Washington, DC: Policy Studies Associates, Inc., 1994, pp. iii-iv.
[31] Funkhouser and Colopy, p. iv.

districts. A 1996 report by Minnesota's legislative auditor's office found a high degree of satisfaction for the state's Post-Secondary Enrollment Options Program. Fewer than one-third of high school administrators described the program as having an "overall negative impact on secondary schools" and more than half said the program increased cooperative efforts between school districts and post-secondary institutions. Finally, 73 percent of participating students said they were "very satisfied" with their experience, and 95 percent of parents of participating students would encourage their children to join the program again.

Despite similarities, important differences remain between the Massachusetts and Minnesota interdistrict choice policies, particularly regarding potential racial and financial impacts. Not only can Minnesota districts refuse transfers because of racial impact, their funding formulas allow only state aid funds to follow transferring students, which account for about 60 percent of total operating expenditures for a typical district. Thus the financial burden of choice on sending districts is lower in Minnesota than in Massachusetts.

CHARTER SCHOOLS

To date, 25 states have authorized nearly 350 publicly financed charter schools as a new and growing alternative to traditional public schools. Indeed, in several Massachusetts towns, charter schools, receiving schools, and sending schools can all be found in close proximity to one another, providing real-life laboratories to evaluate the systemic impact of school choice.

While it is still too early to determine the impact of charter schools on system or student outcomes, they have been tremendously popular among parents and nearly all of them have substantial waiting lists. Two recent studies confirm that these schools are being sought out not by parents of privileged children but by families least well served by conventional public schools. In one sample of 8,400 students, 63 percent were members of minority groups, 55 percent were poor, 19 percent had limited English proficiency, and 19 percent had disabilities that affected their education.[32] In a recent Pioneer Institute report that used demographic data from the Massachusetts Department of Education, researchers found that such schools are serving a higher percentage of low-income (39 percent vs. 25 percent), language minority (14 percent vs. 7 percent), and racial/ethnic minority children (48 percent vs. 21 percent) than traditional public schools in the state, dispelling fears that charter schools would serve a primarily white, affluent population. In addition, 75 percent of parents surveyed reported that their children had become more interested in school and 55 percent said they have become more involved with their children's education at charter schools.[33]

SCHOOL CHOICE AND STUDENT ACHIEVEMENT

After several years of school choice, it is unclear whether such programs improve student achievement. Researchers have yet to provide a definitive answer for several reasons. First, there are many definitions of school choice, ranging from intradistrict public school choice plans to open enrollment policies to private school tax credits. So when we ask whether school choice improves student achievement, we need to be clear about what kind of school choice program we are analyzing. Aside from the diversity of choice programs there is also a diversity of instruments for measuring student achievement.

---

[32] Chester E. Finn, Jr., "Beating Up on Charter Schools," *New York Times,* August 24, 1996, p. 23.
[33] "Massachusetts Charter Schools Profiles, 1995–96 School Year," Boston: Pioneer Institute for Public Policy Research, July 1996.

Second, the school choice system envisioned most famously by Chubb and Moe does not actually exist. No large-scale, unrestricted school choice program has been created by any of the state legislatures. Milwaukee's program is limited to low-income students and includes only 12 schools and fewer than 1,000 students. Indiana has been restricted by court-ordered racial balance requirements and limits its choice programs to privately funded scholarship programs. San Antonio's popular bilingual choice program involves only two schools whose primary aim is not to increase student achievement but rather to immerse students in Latino culture and history.

CHOICE AND COMPETITION

Compared to studies of parent satisfaction or achievement outcomes for choice populations, there has been much less research on the market competition thesis itself, which asserts that inter-school competition will improve school quality for the population at large. That is, the thesis holds that competition between schools or school districts for students will increase school productivity, which means improved student outcomes per unit of cost.

Notable exceptions in this regard are studies by Carolyn M. Hoxby, who uses national data to conduct macroeconomic analyses of the relationship among public and private school competition, school resources, and student outcomes. In the case of public school competition, she finds that increased choice due to greater numbers of separate school districts in a metropolitan area is associated with improved student performance (test scores, educational attainment, and future wages) and lower per pupil costs. In the case of private versus public school competition, she finds that greater private school enrollment within counties improves student performance in public schools (educational attainment and future wages).[34]

These macroeconomic studies of necessity make many assumptions about the nature of the causal linkages between school competition on the one hand and improved student outcomes on the other. In particular, there is little evidence in these studies about the actual mechanisms and processes that produce (or fail to produce) improved education programs in response to competition, which are presumed to precede improvements in student outcomes. It is this type of microeconomic information that this study aims to provide.

---

[34] Carolyn Minter Hoxby, "Does Competition among Public Schools Benefit Students and Taxpayers?" and "Do Private Schools Provide Competition for Public Schools?" *NBER Working Paper Series*, National Bureau of Economic Research, Cambridge, Massachusetts, 1994.

CHAPTER THREE

Study Background and Design

In order to set the stage for our study of the Massachusetts interdistrict choice law, this chapter will outline the history of the Massachusetts choice law, followed by some descriptive data on the growth of the choice populations of students and schools. These basic statistics will include all three Massachusetts choice policies: interdistrict choice, charter schools, and METCO. We will then lay out our study design and briefly describe the types of data we have collected and analyzed to address our principal research questions.

History of the Massachusetts Choice Law

The Massachusetts interdistrict choice law was passed in March 1991 as part of a fiscal recovery act. The first interdistrict choice students began transferring in the fall of 1991. The law required districts to vote to become receiving districts, but they could not prevent transfers out. Starting in 1994, a district has to vote yearly if it does not want to be a receiving district. If a district agrees to receive out-of-district students, it cannot apply any selection criteria to individual students, and the number of transfers in is limited only by school capacity. The law contains no racial restrictions.

The financial provisions in the original choice law established that payment of tuition costs to the district receiving a student should be equal to the full per pupil expenditure as determined by that district. Tuition payments, which at that time were on the order of $5,000 per student (but varied considerably from district to district), were subtracted from the sending district's state aid payments under Chapter 70 of the General Laws. Thus if a district had per pupil expenditures of $5,000 and it received 50 students from another district, it would receive $250,000 in tuition payments, all deducted from the sending district's state aid.[1] If the sending district had a total enrollment of 5,000 students and was receiving $1,000 per pupil in state aid, the loss of these 50 students (1 percent of total enrollment) would cost the district 5 percent of its total state aid ($250,000 from $5 million).

The law produced a great deal of controversy during the first year, particularly in communities that lost a considerable number of choice students. A good example was Brockton, which lost more than 100 students, most of whom transferred to nearby Avon. Gloucester also lost a large number of students that year to nearby Manchester. Both of these sending communities had relatively high rates of low-income families, and Brockton also had a high percentage of minority students.

By the middle of that school year legislation was passed to permit reimbursement for up to 50 percent of a district's state aid losses due to choice. It is estimated that the state paid 60 percent of total choice tuition costs that year.[2] Nonetheless, districts losing large numbers of students still incurred considerable losses in state aid that year.

The continuing controversy over tuition policies led to further changes for the 1992–93 school year. Tuition rates at receiving districts were set at 75 percent of per pupil expenditures, with a cap of $5000, except for special education students for whom the rate

---

[1] Reimbursement for special education students has always been at 100 percent of the receiving district's costs. Special education costs are substantially higher than those for regular students.
[2] Commonwealth of Massachusetts, Executive Office of Education, *School Choice in Massachusetts,* 1994, p. 7.

remained at 100 percent of actual costs. The reimbursement policy was continued, and there were no other major changes made in the choice program that year.

The last major modifications in the choice law occurred in connection with the Education Reform Act of 1993, a major policy initiative to equalize school financing. The Reform Act established a "foundation" budget, defined as the minimum per pupil expenditure for a quality education, which could vary by district (e.g., to compensate for differing poverty levels or wage rates). School districts that were below the foundation level would get additional state aid calculated to bring them to foundation levels over a seven-year period; districts above foundation level would receive smaller amounts of state aid (see chapter 5).

The major change in the choice law involved reimbursement procedures for below foundation districts. Most of these were classified as low wealth by the state, and among this group were most of the larger urban districts with higher concentrations of minority and poverty students. These below foundation districts would be reimbursed for 100 percent of their tuition payments during 1992–93 school year (paid in 1994) and 100 percent of any *increases* in tuition payments thereafter. Districts with spending above foundation level would be eligible for 50 percent reimbursement of tuition payments in the first year in which they lose a particular student and for 25 percent thereafter.

Another change in the choice law was a provision for transportation subsidies for low-income students, that is, students eligible for the free and reduced-price lunch program. This change was partly a response to criticisms that most choice students were predominantly white, even from sending districts with high minority enrollments. Although these funding changes clearly reduced the financial burdens on net sending districts with spending below foundation level, these school districts still pay a portion of tuition costs out of their state aid contributions. For this reason the funding mechanisms of choice in Massachusetts remain controversial.

The choice program has also been controversial for its racial impacts. A report from state senator Arthur Chase's office in 1994 criticized the choice law because it was allowing large numbers of white and non-poverty students to leave districts with high minority and poverty concentrations, thereby "exacerbating minority isolation" in these communities.[3]

TRENDS IN CHOICE PARTICIPATION

There are two levels of participation in the interdistrict choice program, one for students (who can choose to attend school in another district) and one for school districts (that become senders if students leave but must vote to avoid becoming receiving districts). The interdistrict choice program has expanded significantly at both levels during the six years since the choice law was adopted in 1991.

TRENDS IN INTERDISTRICT CHOICE

Table 3–1 shows the trends in the number of interdistrict choice students, both as "head counts" and as full-time equivalents (FTE), as well as the trends in the number of receiving and sending districts. Choice enrollment grew steadily during the first three years of the program, although growth appears to be slowing in the most recent years. For school year 1995–96, interdistrict choice enrollment was approximately 6,800 or 38 percent of the cap (2 percent of the total statewide public school enrollment of about 886,000).

---

[3] Office of Senator Arthur E. Chase, *School Choice in Massachusetts: Good Intentions Gone Awry*, December 1994, p. 24.

The number of receiving districts also expanded rapidly during the early years, but that too has slowed down. While only 89 of the 331 school districts in Massachusetts had become receiving districts as of the 1995–96 school year, there are 206 sending districts statewide, and 220 districts are either sending or receiving districts. Thus two-thirds of Massachusetts school districts are affected to some extent by the choice law.

Table 3–1
Trends in Choice Students and Districts

Year	Total Students	FTE[a]	Receiving Districts	Sending Districts
1991–92	1,000	N/A	32	116
1992–93	3,657[b]	3,208	64	192
1993–94	5,111	4,402	73	199
1994–95	6,219	5,431	85	219
1995–96	6,793	6,038	89	206

Source: The student and district counts are taken from the spring reports for each school year. METCO choice students are not counted here.

[a] Students returning to home school counted only for months attending.
[b] Estimated.

The interdistrict choice student population is not uniform across grade levels, and in fact it is proportionately higher in the secondary grades. In 1994–95 high school grades accounted for more than 3,200 transfers, or about 55 percent of choice students. Twenty percent of choice students were in middle grades six to eight, and the remaining 25 percent are elementary students. Choice students are representative of the general population with respect to gender, however, with choice students divided almost equally between male and female.

We have no precise data on how many choice students enter the choice program directly from private schools. The state data file for 1994–95 indicates that only 8 percent of choice students attended a private or parochial school in the previous school year (1993–94), but this figure excludes any former private school students who had been in the choice program for two or more years.

Tuition transfer payments amounted to $22.5 million in the 1994–95 school year. Since there are far fewer districts receiving than sending students, the average dollar gains or losses are quite different for the two groups. The 85 districts that received students gained an average of $264,000, while the 219 districts that sent students lost an average of $103,000.

The number of transfers is not uniform across districts, and a relatively small number of school districts account for a large portion of the choice population. For example, there are 18 districts with more than 100 choice students enrolled; these districts account for nearly one-half of all choice students. Likewise, 17 districts have more than 100 students transferring out, and they account for more than 40 percent of all choice students. Accordingly, the average tuition payment to these larger net receiving districts was on the order of $600,000 per district and the average loss to larger net sending districts was on the order of $500,000 per district.

Enrollment in Charter Schools and METCO

In addition to the interdistrict choice students, there is a rapidly growing student population in charter schools and a sizable enrollment in the long-standing METCO program.

Although the 22 existing charter schools opened recently (1995 and 1996), charter school enrollment is already approaching that of interdistrict choice enrollment. In 1995–96 there were 15 charter schools and an enrollment of about 2,600 students; in 1996–97 there are 22 operating charter schools and enrollment of 5,465 students.[4] Further, there is a current waiting list of about 3,600 students, and three additional charter schools are set to open in 1997.[5]

The METCO program enrolled nearly 3,200 students in 1995–96, all of whom are minority students (mostly African-American). Nearly all transfer from Boston to 32 surrounding suburban communities; 175 transferred from Springfield to five surrounding suburbs. Of the 37 school districts that receive METCO students, 32 are not participating in the interdistrict choice program—undoubtedly because they are already accepting significant numbers of transfer students from Boston or Springfield. The median METCO enrollment for Boston suburban districts is 70 students, and nine suburbs have more than 100 METCO students enrolled. If we add the districts receiving METCO students in 1995–96 to those receiving interdistrict choice students, a total of 121 districts in Massachusetts voluntarily received transfers from other districts.

Altogether nearly 15,000 Massachusetts students are enrolled in some type of school choice program, leaving their home school system to enroll either in another school district or a charter school.[6] While this is a large number in absolute terms, it nonetheless represents only about 1.6 percent of total statewide public school enrollment. The choice population is likely to grow in coming years if the statutory cap on charter schools is lifted or more districts are required to participate in the interdistrict choice program.

---

[4] These data are taken from Massachusetts Department of Education, *The Massachusetts Charter School Initiative, 1996 Report,* published in January 1997.
[5] Both the number of charter schools and charter school enrollment are currently capped, at 25 and three-quarters of 1 percent of statewide public school enrollment, respectively.
[6] Although most charter school students attend schools in their home towns, these schools operate as independent school districts.

SUMMARY OF STUDY DESIGN

The major purpose of this study is to test several of the assumptions and arguments made by proponents and critics of school choice policies. We will briefly describe the methodology and data we have employed to study each of these research questions.

SOCIAL, RACIAL, AND FINANCIAL EFFECTS

The questions of social, racial, and financial effects of choice are explored in chapter 4 using statewide data from the Massachusetts Department of Education for the 1994–95 school year. One set of data provides a "profile" of all school districts in the state, which includes the demographic characteristics of communities, total school enrollment by race, school expenditures, school socioeconomic status (SES), such as percent eligible for free or reduced-price lunch, and a series of academic characteristics such as attendance, dropout rates, college plans, and achievement test scores.

In order to assess racial and financial effects, a data set was also obtained from the state containing information on all choice students in the 1994–95 school year. The choice data include the receiving district, the sending district, race, grade, gender, district attended the prior year, and the amount of tuition paid for that student. By summing these data for receiving and sending districts and merging it with the district profile data, it was possible to compute racial composition with and without choice students as well as tuition gains/losses for each district.

The analysis of social and academic characteristics of choice students also relied on some additional data collected for this study only: the student and parent survey collected in our case study districts (described below), and a special statewide choice data set (1995–96) that included achievement test scores and some questionnaire items for 10th graders.

THE MARKET COMPETITION THESIS

The test of the market competition thesis presented in chapter 5 is based on both case study information and state data. For the case studies we selected a non-random sample of 10 pairs of school districts, one being a net receiving district with more than 100 transfers in and one being a net sending district with the largest number of transfers to that receiver (all but one sender also had 100 or more transfers out). This sample represents more than half of the largest senders and receivers in the state.

Table 3–2 shows the actual number of choice students received or sent by each case study district for 1994–95, as well as their total enrollment that year. Several districts have more than 200 choice students transferring in, including Acton-Boxborough, Avon, and Holliston, which were the largest receivers in the state that year. Only one sending district, Springfield, has more than 200 choice students out, but both Brockton and Fitchburg have close to 190; these are three of the four largest sending districts in the state for that year.[7]

It is worth noting that Brockton, Gloucester, Lynn, and Springfield had voted against receiving students as of the 1994–95 school year, in spite of heavy choice losses. Gloucester did become a receiving district at the high school level as of 1996–97.

Geographically, the case study districts are spread over the eastern two-thirds of the state, and the district sizes range from very small to very large. Avon is smallest with an enrollment of 795, and Springfield is largest at 24,000—the second largest district in Massachusetts after Boston. While all of the receiving districts are relatively small, with enrollments ranging from about 800 to 3300, there is considerable variation in the senders, ranging from 1300 to

---

[7] Triton at 219 is the second largest sender after Springfield.

24,000. On average, however, sending districts are larger than receiving districts.

Table 3–2
Case Study Districts, 1994–95

District	Number of Choice In	Number of Choice Out	District Enrollment
NET RECEIVERS			
Acton-Boxborough	284	11	1,920
Avon	228	0	795
Harvard	183	0	1,047
Holliston	313	13	2,964
Lunenburg	133	39	1,786
Manchester	138	8	857
Marblehead	140	1	2,776
Uxbridge	136	46	1,920
Hampden-Wilbraham	107	2	3,352
Pentucket	198	52	3,011
NET SENDERS			
Brockton	0	188	14,346
Fitchburg	66	187	5,024
Gloucester	0	145	3,869
Haverhill	26	154	7,930
Hopkinton	36	98	1,895
Leominster	65	171	5,642
Lynn	0	154	13,125
Maynard	33	135	1,301
Northbridge	79	105	2,020
Springfield	0	258	24,063

Note: Districts are categorized as net senders if they have more transfers out than in and as net receivers if they have more transfers in than out.

All but three districts serve grades K to 12 and draw their resident students from a single community. The three exceptions (all receivers) are the regional districts of Acton-Boxborough (junior-senior high school), Hampden-Wilbraham (K–12), and Pentucket, a regional K–12 system serving the communities of Groveland, Merrimack, and West Newbury.

We conducted site visits at 19 of these 20 districts and interviewed superintendents, school committee members, principals, and business managers during the first half of 1996.[8] The questionnaire emphasized the reasons for choice transfers in or out, the specific impact of choice gains or losses on school programs and policies, and views of the choice law (see appendix B for the interview form).

In order to validate the interview findings, we used official enrollment, tuition, and expenditure measures for these 20 districts drawn from statewide profile data and choice reports. The choice reports provided enrollment counts and tuition payments for each school year from 1992–93 to 1995–96, allowing an assessment of choice and tuition trends during this four-year period.

Beyond our case study sample, there are only nine other districts in Massachusetts that have 100 or more transfers out. We used these additional net sending districts to conduct a special trend analysis to test the robustness of certain findings based on the case study sample of 10 net sending districts. In particular, we examined choice enrollment trends between 1992–93 and 1995–96.

These additional districts are listed in table 3–3 along with their choice and total enrollments. We note that five of these districts are also receiving districts with significant numbers of transfers in, but

---

[8] One sending district did not wish to participate in the study.

that four districts—Lowell, Pittsfield, Salem, and Worcester—had voted against becoming receivers as of the 1995–96 school year.

Table 3–3
Other Net Sending Districts with 100 or More Choice Transfers Out, 1994–95

District	Number of Choice In	Number of Choice Out	District Enrollment
Amesbury	83	142	2,709
Ayer	73	105	1,389
Clinton	40	102	1,807
Lowell	0	152	14,693
Milford	105	120	3,828
Pittsfield	0	113	6,854
Salem	0	104	4,757
Worcester	0	109	22,568
Triton	103	219	3,032

FAMILY AND RESIDENT ATTITUDES

Finally, the data for the views of parents, students, and citizens (see chapter 6) are based on three surveys, two of which were designed specifically for this study.

For the parent and student surveys, we randomly selected between 40 and 50 choice families from each of the 10 net receiving districts in the case study sample. After obtaining appropriate informed consent, we conducted structured telephone interviews with all consenting parents. We interviewed a total 309 parents from the 10 receiving districts for an average of 31 per school during the first six months of 1996. All but two districts had 25 or more parents.

Students from consenting choice families who were in grade 8 and higher were given a brief written questionnaire in a group setting during our site visits. A total of 213 students completed the questionnaire for an average of 21 per school. Our parent and student response rate was approximately 70 percent of sampled families (see appendix B for questionnaires).

The citizen survey was sponsored by the Pioneer Institute as part of a separate study of school choice. A total of 700 Massachusetts adult residents were interviewed during July 1996, which included oversampling of 200 parents in the 10 largest cities and 100 minority parents in Boston. We are relying on a portion of the results from that survey.[9] In particular, we use the citizen survey to assess the overall support or opposition to choice, including urban and minority citizens, and we discuss the implications of support or opposition by race to help interpret the racial impacts of the choice program.

---

[9] See *Massachusetts Attitudes Concerning School Choice,* Boston: Pioneer Institute for Public Policy Research, August 1996.

CHAPTER FOUR

SOCIAL, RACIAL, AND FINANCIAL IMPACTS OF CHOICE

A common criticism of unrestricted school choice is that it will increase the social and racial segregation of students, particularly in and around urban school districts, and will bring further financial hardships to already disadvantaged schools. Thus whatever advantage might accrue to choice students would be outweighed by greater disadvantage to those remaining behind in sending districts.

There is some support for the social and financial effect thesis in a study of the Massachusetts choice program by Richard Fossey, cited in chapter 2.[1] Using choice enrollment as of the fall of 1992, he compared the average family income, per pupil expenditures, and achievement test scores for pairs of sending and receiving districts with 20 or more choice students transferring from one district to another. He found that, on the average, sending districts had lower family incomes, expenditures, and test scores than the receiving districts. However, the Fossey study did not have data on individual choice students, so he could not compare choice students with nonchoice students, nor could he calculate the effect of transfers on changes in district characteristics (e.g., the effect of transfers on per pupil expenditures).

---

[1] Richard Fossey, "Open Enrollment in Massachusetts: Why Families Choose," *Educational Evaluation and Policy Analysis*, Vol. 16, No. 3 (Fall 1994): 320–334.

A related issue raised by critics of the Massachusetts choice policy concerns tuition payments, which must be paid by sending districts to receiving districts for all choice students. The argument is that net sending districts as compared to net receivers tend to be disadvantaged with respect to education spending, so that, in effect, choice takes needed funds away from poor districts and gives them to the rich. It should be noted that there are provisions for reimbursing net senders for some portion of the tuition payments, particularly if the sender is receiving state foundation aid. Nonetheless, a net sending district receives less state aid than it would if there were no choice law.

This chapter explores the effects of the Massachusetts interdistrict choice program on the social, racial, and financial status of school districts. For most of this analysis we include all school districts in the state that are affected by interdistrict choice, whether receiver, sender, or both, using data from the Massachusetts Department of Education. Some of these analyses are also replicated for our sample of 20 case study districts to determine whether they are representative of the state as a whole. For the assessment of racial representation, we also include the statewide populations of METCO and charter school students.

Defining Impact

We can distinguish several potential effects of interdistrict school choice on the social and racial compositions of student populations. The first is that net receiving districts will be more affluent and have fewer minority students than net sending districts. We have already cited some evidence that this may be true in Massachusetts (e.g., Fossey). The second is that choice students will not be representative of their peers in the sending districts, that they will have higher SES and be less minority. Finally, it is often assumed—but not demonstrated—that the combination of these two possibilities will result in a significant adverse impact on the social and racial composition of sending districts.

It is not logically necessary that one imply the others. For example, if the first two conditions are true—choice students are high SES and mostly white and they transfer from high minority sender to low minority receiver—the magnitude of the effect on the sending district depends on the number of choice students and the enrollment in the sending district. If the number of choice students is small compared to the sending district's enrollment, then there may be no *significant* adverse racial impact on the sending district. Additionally, that same group of choice students may still have a higher minority percentage than the receiving district, such that choice has significant *positive* racial impact on the receiver.

A similar scenario applies to financial effects. While all senders make tuition payments to receivers, if a sender is much larger than a receiver, then the budget impact might be relatively small for the sender but relatively large for the receiver. Moreover, a sender can also become a receiver, and therefore tuition income might offset tuition outlays.

Given the nature of our data, we can estimate all of these effects although not necessarily statewide. For the first type of effect, we can compare the social, racial, and selected academic characteristics for all sending and receiving districts. For the second type of effect, we can compare the racial composition of the interdistrict choice, METCO, and charter school populations to the total state population, and for selected social characteristics we can compare interdistrict choice students to their sending and receiving schools.

Most important, by knowing the race of all individual interdistrict choice students, we can determine the *magnitude* of racial impacts on both sending and receiving districts. To our knowledge, this analysis has never been carried out for the Massachusetts interdistrict choice program. Likewise, we can go beyond a simple analysis of tuition payments by senders; we can determine the magnitude of financial effects on sending and receiving districts that are due to choice.

Because of the importance of potential racial impact, we want to be clear about the significance of the second and third types of racial effects. If interdistrict choice students are less minority than the relevant sending districts but there is no significant impact on the sending district's racial composition—because the choice population is too small—then our conclusion about racial impacts must be carefully stated. Such a finding would confirm one aspect of the critics' argument about racial impacts but disconfirm another. This finding would alleviate concerns about segregative effects of choice, but it would raise concerns about the motivations of choice parents and students for changing school districts. That issue will be addressed specifically in chapter 6 using our survey of choice students and parents.

Social, Racial, and Academic Characteristics

A comparison of the social, racial, and academic characteristics of sending versus receiving districts is accomplished using the statewide profile of school districts for the 1994–95 school year. Given the possibility that larger school districts may have larger choice enrollments simply because of their size, we also break out these characteristics according to the percentage of total enrollment who are choice transfers (in or out). In addition to comparing senders and receivers, this lets us determine whether school districts with higher choice impact (either receiving or sending) differ from those with lower impact.

These comparisons are shown in table 4–1. Comparing all sending districts to all receiving districts, there are only very small differences in average SES or academic characteristics. The average percent of adults with BA degrees in the communities, average attendance rates, and average suspension rates are identical; most of the other differences are very small and not significant. Note that the average percent minority (black or Hispanic) is only 7 percent among all senders and 5 percent among all receivers. Finally, receivers score slightly higher than senders in 10th grade reading and math scores (4 and 3 points, respectively), but the differences are not statistically significant.[2]

Likewise, there are few differences among senders with lower or higher rates of choice transfers out. There are larger SES differences between senders and receivers, however, where choice students constitute more than 2 percent of total enrollment. High-impact receivers are 5 points higher in percent with BA degrees, $41,000 higher in property value, 6 points lower in poverty, 4 points lower in minority enrollment, and 11 to 13 points higher in 10th grade test scores. Because of the small number of districts in these categories, however, none of these differences are statistically significant.

What about differences between choice students and their respective sending and receiving districts? Unfortunately, we do not have statewide data on choice students for most of the items in table 4–1, with the exception of race, which is discussed in the next section. We do have a number of SES and academic characteristics for the sample of 20 case study districts. This sample also has the advantage that all districts have at least 100 choice students either in or out, and that each sending district in the sample is the largest sender to one of the receiving districts.

---

[2] The district-level standard deviation is approximately 78 for both tests.

Table 4–1
Characteristics of All Sending and Receiving Districts, 1994–95

	Rate of Choice Transfers[a]		
	Under 2%	2% or More	All districts
SENDING DISTRICTS			
COMMUNITY SES			
Mean Income ($)	49,367	46,217	48,765
% BA Degree	27	23	26
Property Value ($)	531,543	523,191	530,014
SCHOOL SES			
% Poverty	16	17	16
% Minority[b]	7	7	7
% Black	3	2	3
ACADEMIC			
% Attending	94	94	94
% Suspended	5	5	5
% Dropout	9	8	9
% Planning to Attend 4–Year College	47	47	47
10th Reading	1,324	1,321	1,324
10th Math	1,319	1,318	1,319
(N)	(174)	(39)	(213)
RECEIVING DISTRICTS			
COMMUNITY SES			
Mean Income ($)	41,670	50,430	47,664
% BA Degree	19	28	26
Property Value ($)	447,006	564,838	528,795
SCHOOL SES			
% Poverty	22	11	15
% Minority[b]	7	3	5
% Black	2	2	2
ACADEMIC			
% Attending	94	94	94
% Suspended	5	5	5
% Dropout	11	7	8
% Planning to Attend 4–Year College	45	50	48
10th Reading	1,315	1,334	1,328
10th Math	1,307	1,329	1,322
(N)	(26)	(59)	(85)

[a] Percent of total enrollment transferring in or out.
[b] African-American or Hispanic only.

Table 4–2 provides a comparison of the same SES and academic characteristics for the 10 sending districts and the 10 receiving districts in the case study sample. The table also has a third column that shows several SES and academic characteristics for a sample of choice families and students who attend school in one of the 10 receiving districts, most of whom transfer from one of the 10 sending districts.

Table 4–2
Characteristics of Large Choice Districts and Students, 1994–95

	Sending Districts	Receiving Districts	Choice[a] Families
COMMUNITY SES			
Mean Income ($)	41,862	55,139	53,000
% BA Degree	19	33	48
Property Value ($)	403,332	621,455	N/A
SCHOOL SES			
% Poverty	32	7	-
% Minority[b]	22	3	6
% Black	9	2	4
ACADEMIC			
% Attending	93	95	-
% Suspended	6	4	-
% Dropout	16	7	-
% Planning to Attend 4–Year College	53	69	79
10th Reading	1286	1386	1380
10th Math	1273	1377	1374
(Number of districts)	(10)	(10)	
(Number of parents/students)			(309/213)

[a] Income and % BA from parent survey (N=309); race and college plans from student survey (N=213); test scores from 1996 state administration (N=216).
[b] African-American or Hispanic only.

Unlike table 4–1, this comparison shows substantial differences in SES and academic characteristics of large sending and receiving districts (100 or more choice students in or out). Considering community SES characteristics, these large receiving districts are more affluent with family income and per pupil property valuation averaging about $13,000 and $218,000 higher than senders, respectively, and with adults having nearly twice the rate of college graduates (33 versus 19 percent). These large receiving districts also have lower poverty rates (7 versus 32 percent) and lower percentages of minority students among their school populations (3 versus 22 percent). With regard to academic characteristics, large receivers have about half the dropout rate (7 versus 16 percent), and a higher percentage of receiving district seniors are planning to attend four-year colleges (69 versus 53 percent). There are no significant differences between large sending and receiving districts for attendance rates and rates of suspension for disciplinary problems.

What about the characteristics of choice families compared to their sending and receiving districts? Table 4–2 also compares average characteristics of choice families with children attending these large receiving districts with the average sending and receiving school populations. Choice family incomes are somewhat lower on average than receiving districts but much higher than the sending district, and the choice parent college graduation rate is 15 percentage points higher than the receiving district average. Consistent with their parents' education, the percentage of choice students planning to attend four-year college is also 10 points higher than that for receiving districts. Finally, average 10th grade test scores of choice students are much higher than the average student's in large sending districts and about the same as their peers in receiving districts.

Interestingly, we note that the percent minority among choice students is higher than for all receiving district students, but still considerably lower than that for sending districts. The same holds for the percent African-American; it is higher for choice students than for receivers but it is still lower than for senders (it is about halfway between the two). This raises the possibility that the interdistrict choice program may actually benefit integration for some receiving schools.

There is strong evidence here that choice families on average are indeed higher SES and less minority than families in sending districts. In fact, choice students even exceed receiving district students in both parents' education and student college aspirations, but they are slightly lower in family income and about the same in test scores. This particular pattern suggests that children in choice families are achieving at a much higher rate than the average sending school students and also have a much stronger interest in higher education—even greater than the average receiver family—but may not necessarily have the resources to afford private school tuition at either the secondary or college level. This may well have implications for their motivation for involvement in the choice program, which we will explore in greater depth in chapter 6.

What about the impact of choice transfers on the social and academic characteristics of both the sending and receiving schools? Unfortunately, we do not have complete SES or academic data for choice students, and therefore we cannot the calculate the effect of choice on changes in sending and receiving districts' social composition in the same way as for racial impacts. It is possible, however, to compare the 10th grade test scores of choice students in our 20 case study districts with test scores in their respective sending and receiving districts, and thereby estimate the approximate magnitude of such effects.[3]

---

[3] The test score data for comparing choice students with their receiving and sending schools were derived by merging the statewide choice file with the statewide school profile file, but profile data do not include the number of 10th

Figure 4–1A compares the differences in mean reading scores in our 10 receiving and 10 sending districts, where the means are computed for the total 10th grade population in each school. A positive difference means that the average receiving district student scores higher than the average student in that district's largest sender. Figure 4–1B compares the mean reading scores for choice students in these receivers to the mean scores in their respective senders; a positive difference means choice students score higher than their sending district peers.

Three observations can be made from these comparisons. First, figure 4–1A shows that not all receivers have significantly higher reading scores than their largest senders; the differences for Pentucket-Haverhill, Avon-Brockton, and Uxbridge-Northbridge are small, and in the case of Holliston-Hopkinton, the sender has higher reading scores than the receiver. Second, figure 4–1B reveals that choice students are not always the academic "cream" of their sending district, with three comparisons showing choice students having lower reading scores than their peers and one comparison showing almost no difference. Finally, only four of the ten pairs have a pattern that coincides with the critics' position of a low-achieving sender that loses high-achieving students to a high-achieving receiver (Acton-Maynard, Harvard-Leominster, Pentucket-Haverhill, and Lunenburg-Fitchburg).

It seems clear from these results that the social and academic impacts of choice are much more complex than is portrayed by either critics or proponents of choice policies. On the one hand, the data support the critics' views that choice students *on average* tend to be more affluent and academically talented than the students in the

---

graders who took the test in each district. The merged data provided 10th grade test scores for approximately 80 percent of the 10th grade choice students in the aggregate.

Social, Racial, and Financial Impacts of Choice 57

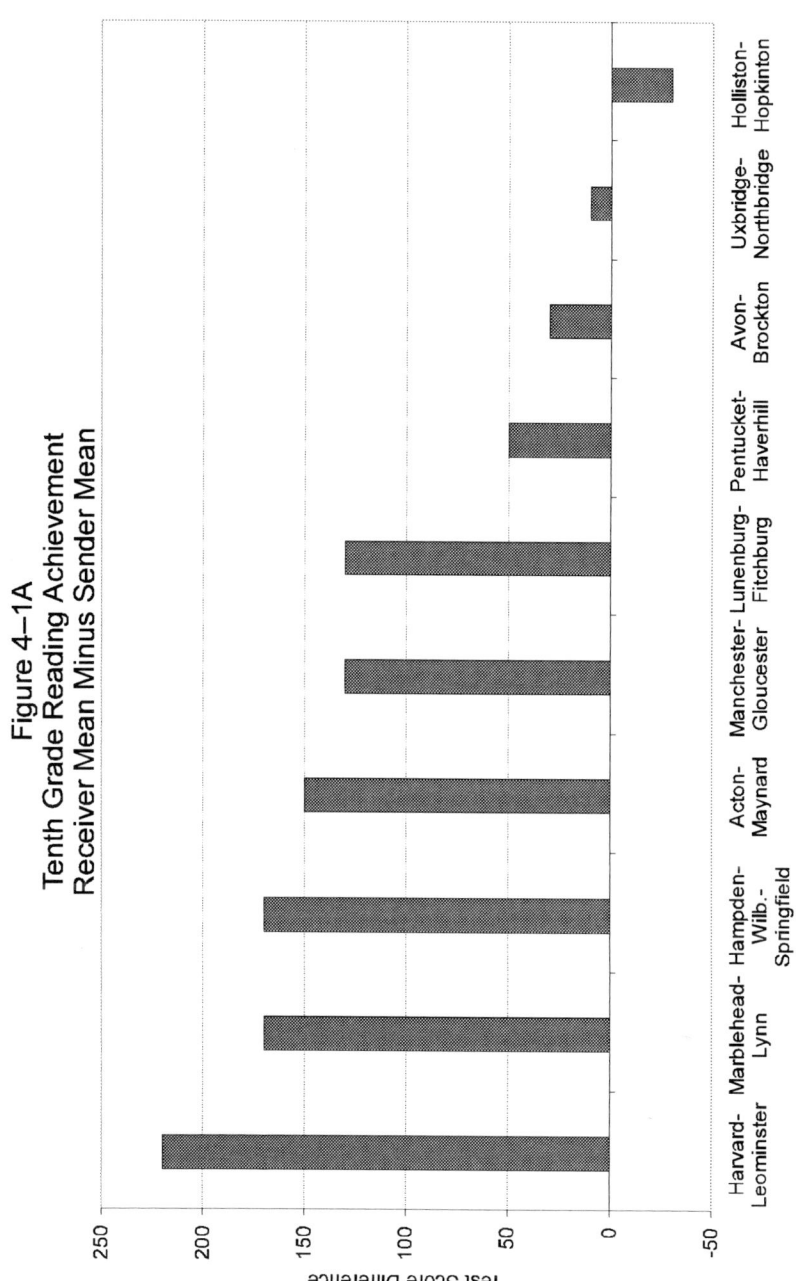

average sending district, and they migrate from lower SES, lower achieving districts to more affluent and higher achieving districts. On the other hand, this "average" depiction masks a much more complex picture, in which individual districts do not fit the average profile.

RACIAL IMPACTS

Having shown that, on average, large sending districts tend to have higher minority enrollments than large receivers, the assessment of racial impacts in this section will focus on two questions. First, how does the racial composition of various choice populations compare with the statewide population? For addressing this question we include interdistrict public school choice, METCO, and charter school populations. Second, what is the impact of the interdistrict choice program on the racial makeup of sending and receiving districts, that is, is it having segregative effects?

RACIAL REPRESENTATION IN CHOICE POPULATIONS

One complication in making a comparison between the racial composition of the regular interdistrict choice and the statewide populations concerns Boston and its suburbs. Almost none of the Boston suburban districts within reasonable commuting distance participate in interdistrict choice. At the same time Boston comprises nearly half of the statewide African-American enrollment and a sizable portion of the state Hispanic population.

Some Boston families who want to leave the Boston public schools have two choices. Subject to space availability, some minority families can choose a suburban METCO district, and some families can choose among several charter schools. In order to assess the racial equability of choice in Massachusetts, therefore, it seems more reasonable to compare statewide racial composition to the compositions of all these choice programs.

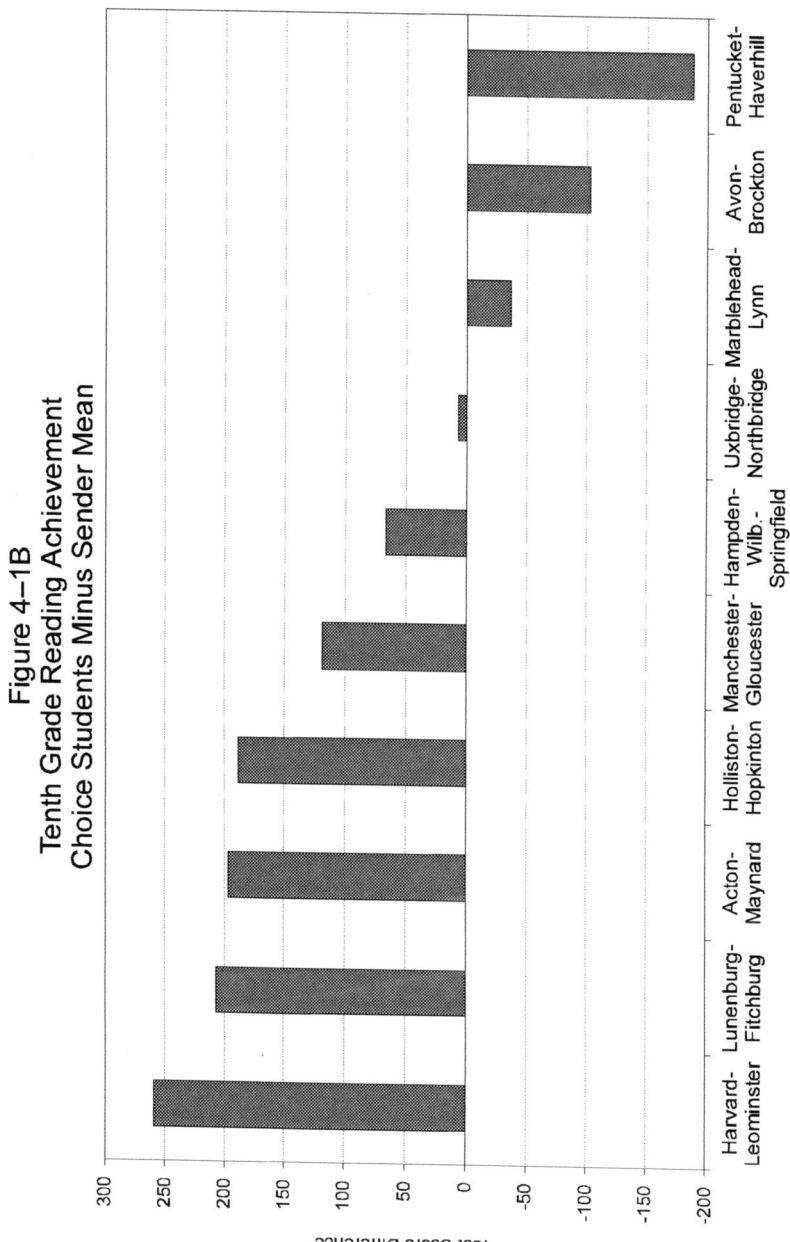

Figure 4-1B
Tenth Grade Reading Achievement
Choice Students Minus Sender Mean

Table 4-3 compares the statewide racial composition (with and without Boston) with the racial composition of interdistrict choice, METCO, and charter school students. While the interdistrict choice population is disproportionately white compared to the state enrollment, it is less so when Boston is excluded. Even so, interdistrict choice students are about 4.5 percent black and Hispanic compared to a statewide school population (less Boston) that is about 13 percent black and Hispanic. On the other hand, the METCO program has a very high African-American enrollment, while the charter school program overrepresents both black and Hispanic students compared to statewide figures.

Table 4-3
Racial/Ethnic Composition of Choice Populations Compared to Statewide Public School Enrollment, 1995-96

	Inter-district Choice[a]	METCO	Charter Schools	All Choice	State	State Less Boston
White	92	0	52	58	79	84
Black	2	86	23	27	8	5
Hispanic	2	8	18	9	9	8
Asian	1	2	2	2	4	3
Other	<1	1	1	<1	<1	<1
Unknown	2	2	—	2	—	—
(N)	(6,219)	(3,194)	(5,465)	(14,878)	(895,881)	(834,392)

[a] 1994-95 school year.

Considering all programs, the total choice population in Massachusetts is reasonably representative of Hispanic, Asian, and other minority groups, and it overrepresents African-American students compared to statewide enrollment. While this analysis is not intended to downplay the underrepresentation of minority students in the interdistrict choice program, it is important to stress that, from the standpoint of state policy, minority students are fully represented in the three choice programs created by the state.

THE RACIAL IMPACT OF INTERDISTRICT CHOICE

Although the interdistrict choice population is somewhat less minority than the relevant statewide population (excluding Boston), it does not necessarily follow that choice must have a significant impact on the racial composition of either net sending or receiving districts. The critical issue is the number of choice students relative to the total sending or receiving district population. We shall show, in fact, that currently choice has no significant negative impact on the racial balance of sending districts and has a slightly positive impact on receiving districts.

Our first measure of racial impact is to examine the effect of racial or poverty composition on the size of choice enrollment. That is, is the racial or poverty composition of districts related to the number of choice students transferring in or out, relative to the size of a district? We determined this effect by first counting the net choice enrollment in each district (transfers in minus transfers out, since some districts have both), then expressing this count as a percentage of total district enrollment, and finally tabulating this percentage into several categories of racial or poverty composition (under 5 percent minority, over 25 percent, etc.). A positive percentage indicates a net receiving district, while a negative percentage indicates a net sending district.

Figure 4–2 shows the effect of choice on enrollment by racial and poverty composition. Looking at the sign of the percentages, we see that school districts over 16 percent minority or over 21 percent poverty tend to be net senders, while districts with lower minority and poverty concentrations tend to be net receivers. In addition, we note that the effect of race is stronger than the effect of poverty; for example, for districts over 25 percent minority, the effect of choice is a loss of 1.3 percent of enrollment, while districts over 30 percent poverty show a loss of only 0.3 percent of enrollment.

The largest effect of choice on enrollment occurs for districts that are 16 to 25 percent minority, but even here the effect of choice is to reduce enrollment by less than 2 percentage points. These small impacts on enrollment have major implications for the impact on racial composition, to which we now turn.

Our second and more important measure of racial impact is to calculate the effect of choice on the actual racial composition of districts. We did this by first counting the number of choice students who transfer into or out of each school district by race. The district enrollment is then adjusted by adding transfers out and subtracting transfers in, by race, which results in the total "resident" enrollment by race.[4] We then estimate the effect of choice on racial composition by subtracting the actual percent white or minority from the "resident" percent white or minority. Basically, this is the change in racial composition if all choice students were returned to their home or resident school districts. We also tabulate these changes according to the size of the school district, because we have already seen that the overall effect of choice is small relative to total enrollments.

Figure 4–3 shows the change in racial composition due to choice transfers for sending districts only, further classified according to district size. We see that the overall effect of choice losses for all sending districts combined (right-most bars) is to reduce the percent white by less than one-tenth of 1 point (-.08%), to raise the percent

---

[4] This resident enrollment is somewhat hypothetical, since if there were no choice law some of these students would return to private or parochial schools. The inclusion of all students in our calculation is conservative, however, because it tends to inflate the racial impact on senders.

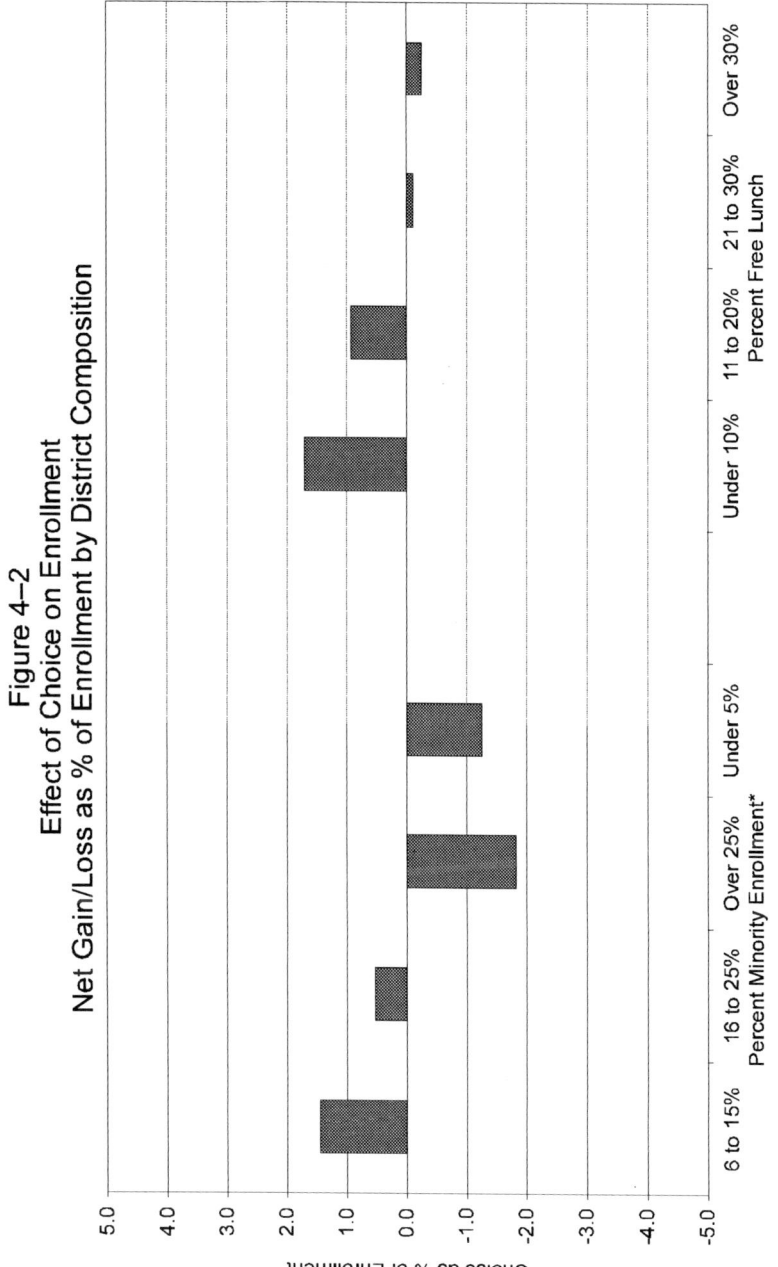

Figure 4–2
Effect of Choice on Enrollment
Net Gain/Loss as % of Enrollment by District Composition

*Minority defined as African-American or Hispanic.

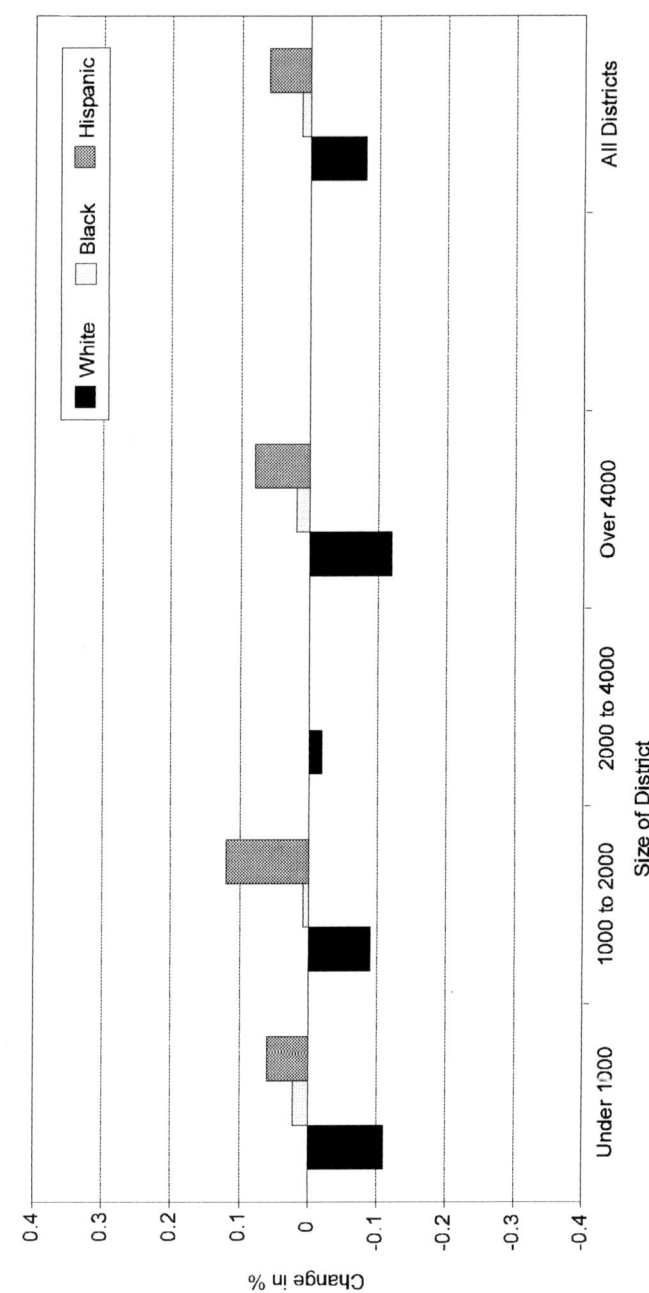

Figure 4-3
Effect of Choice on Composition of Senders
Change in % White, Black, Hispanic

black by only one-hundredth of 1 point (.01%), and to raise the percent Hispanic by less than one-tenth of 1 point (.06%).

Considering sending districts with more than 4000 in total enrollment, which also tend to have the highest minority concentrations, the effect of choice lowers the percent white by just over one-tenth of 1 point (-.12%) and raises the percent Hispanic by just .08. The largest effect occurs in the 1000 to 2000 enrollment category, where the percent Hispanic is raised by just .12. The percentage of African-American students is virtually unaffected in all enrollment categories.

The race and ethnic effects are somewhat larger for receiving districts, as shown in figure 4–4, although in no case does an effect approach even one-half of 1 percent for any size category. More importantly, the effects are generally positive, in that they *improve* the racial balance of receiving districts relative to state averages. That is, for all receiving districts combined, the net effect of choice *lowers* the percent white in receivers by .13 and *raises* the percent Hispanic by .1, which is in the same direction as sending districts. The reason that the effects of choice are in the same direction for both sending and receiving districts has to do with the composition of the choice population. While the choice population has a higher percentage of white students than the average sending district, at the same time it has a higher percentage of minority students than the average receiving district. Thus the effect of choice is to slightly reduce the white and slightly increase the minority composition of both sending and receiving districts.

Again, there is some variation in racial impact according to the average size of receiving districts. As was the case for sending districts, the largest effects on percent white occur for the largest and smallest districts, where the effect of choice is to lower the percent white by about two-tenths of 1 percentage point. The largest impact

Figure 4-4
Effect of Choice on Composition of Receivers
Change in % White, Black, & Hispanic

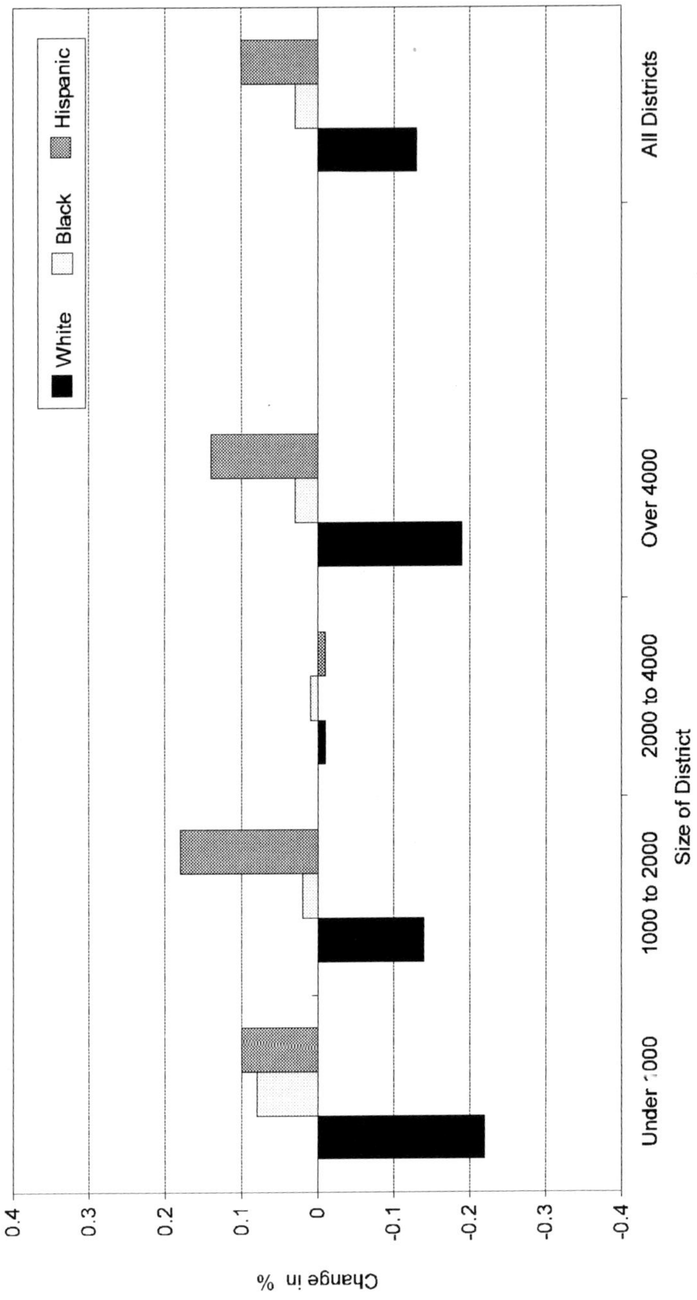

on black composition occurs for the smallest receiving districts, where the percent black is raised by .08—a positive effect that is larger than any negative effect of choice on the black enrollment of sending districts. The largest effect of choice on the percent Hispanic composition occurs for districts in the 1000 to 2000 enrollment range, where we see that choice raises the percent Hispanic by .18.

We can perhaps better illustrate the racial impacts of choice if we examine the magnitude and direction of these effects for individual sending and receiving districts. To make this analysis most relevant to policy, we show the impact of choice on the racial composition of 17 sending districts with more than 100 transfers out and 18 receiving districts with more than 100 transfers in.[5] These 35 districts account for nearly one-half of the total choice population.

Table 4–4 makes it clear that the impacts of choice on segregation or integration are generally very small. It is true that sending districts with the largest choice losses include many with high minority concentrations, while the receiving districts with the largest choice gains are all less than 10 percent minority. But it is also true that some of the largest senders have very low minority enrollments, such as Triton, Gloucester, Northbridge, and Amesbury. It is interesting that the largest sender, Springfield, has the highest minority enrollment, but that the second largest, Triton, has the lowest minority enrollment. In other words, there are clearly factors other than high minority enrollments that lead to large losses of choice students.

The most meaningful information in the table, however, is contained in the last column, which shows negligible effects on the

---

[5] We have dropped two vocational districts, Minuteman and Greater Lawrence, which have 188 transfers in and 133 transfers out, respectively, because these districts already draw from large areas composed of many separate school districts. There is a significant drop of 4 percent white (and a corresponding increase in percent Hispanic) due to choice transfers out of Greater Lawrence.

racial composition of sending districts. Among the largest senders, the greatest racial impact occurs for Springfield, but the effect on its racial composition is less than one-tenth of 1 percent. In spite of the large absolute number of transfers out, the effect in Springfield is to increase the percent minority (black and Hispanic) by only seven-tenths of one percentage point. The reason for this small effect is that Springfield's total enrollment is very large (about 24,000) compared to the transfers out, so that the transfers have a very small effect on the racial makeup of the remaining population.

Interestingly, the largest racial effect for receiving districts occurs for Avon, which shows an increase of 1.2 percent minority due to choice. This is because the students choosing Avon, most of whom are from Brockton, have a higher minority proportion than the Avon resident population. Note that the effect of choice on Brockton's racial composition is negligible. This result clearly demonstrates that in some cases choice can actually improve the racial composition of receiving districts. All of the remaining receivers show negligible or no effects of choice on racial composition, the absolute values of which are less than or equal to three-tenths of 1 percent.

The Financial Impact of Choice

The final type of impact assessed in this chapter concerns the financial and economic effects of choice. Does the choice law lead to a reverse Robin Hood effect, whereby affluent receiving districts gain at the expense of poor sending districts, leaving them significantly more disadvantaged and unable to make the type of program improvements necessary to reverse their losses? To answer this question we not only want to examine the size of the financial impacts but also the relationship between the magnitude of the impact and the racial or poverty composition of districts.

Our analysis of the financial or economic impact of choice has some parallels to the analysis of racial impact. We estimate the size of the financial effect by first calculating net tuition gains or losses for a district in 1994–95 (choice tuition received minus choice tuition paid out), and we express this net tuition as a percentage of total district expenditures.[6] We then tabulate the percentage effects according to both racial and poverty composition categories, and we also show the financial effects for the largest sending and receiving districts.

Figure 4–5 shows the financial impact of net choice tuition income or payments as a percentage of total expenditures. Positive percentages mean increased expenditures as a result of choice, while negative percentages mean lower expenditures. As we saw in figure 4–2, there is a slight relationship between percent minority enrollment or percent poverty and financial impact, although districts with the highest minority concentrations have losses that are half the size of losses in districts with the next highest concentrations (-.6% versus –1.2%). Also, the effect of race is stronger than the effect of poverty.

But the most important story told by figure 4–5 is that all of the financial effects are very small—less than 1 percent of total expenditures gained for all categories of net receiving districts and a maximum of 1.2 percent lost for all categories of net sending districts. The reason that the financial losses for net senders are smaller than their enrollment losses (figure 4–2) is that many are below foundation districts and are receiving extra state aid to raise their spending levels to foundation minimums (see the discussion of the foundation budget in chapter 5). This is not to say that losses from tuition payments

---

[6] Total expenditures for all districts for 1994–95 were not available at the writing of this report, so 1993–94 expenditures are used instead. Since 1993–94 total expenditures are generally smaller than 1994–95, especially for below-foundation districts, the effect of this procedure is to inflate the percentage effects to some extent.

Table 4-4
Racial/Ethnic Impact of Choice for Largest Senders and Receivers, 1994-95

District	Number of Transfers	Actual % Minority[a]	% Minority Without Choice	Change in % Minority
SENDERS WITH MORE THAN 100 TRANSFERS OUT				
Springfield	253	67.2	66.5	0.7
Triton	219	1.3	1.3	0.0
Fitchburg	185	30.4	29.8	0.6
Brockton	175	43.3	43.0	0.3
Leominster	164	18.4	18.2	0.2
Lynn	154	34.5	34.2	0.3
Haverhill	153	16.4	16.1	0.3
Lowell	152	24.9	24.7	0.2
Gloucester	145	1.8	1.7	0.1
Amesbury	142	1.3	1.4	−0.1
Maynard	130	5.9	5.5	0.4
Milford	118	8.4	8.3	0.1
Pittsfield	110	9.4	9.3	0.1
Northbridge	105	2.4	2.6	−0.2
Salem	104	25.7	25.3	0.4
Ayer	103	23.0	22.6	0.4
Worcester	103	34.1	33.9	0.2
RECEIVERS WITH MORE THAN 100 TRANSFERS IN				
Holliston	306	2.0	2.0	0.0
Acton-Boxborough	284	2.4	2.6	−0.2
Avon	213	9.9	8.7	1.2
Pentucket	198	1.1	0.8	0.3
Nashoba	191	4.4	4.1	0.3
Harvard	183	2.1	2.0	0.1
Newburyport	176	1.3	1.3	0.0
Hamilton-Wenham	174	1.2	1.1	0.1
Berkshire Hills	147	3.5	3.8	−0.3
Marblehead	140	4.0	4.0	0.0
Manchester	138	0.6	0.6	0.0
Uxbridge	136	0.6	0.6	0.0
Lunenburg	133	2.2	2.0	0.2
Hampden-Wilbraham	130	3.1	3.0	0.1
Masconomet	116	1.9	2.0	−0.1
Southwick-Tolland	106	2.5	2.6	−0.1
Milford	103	8.4	8.3	0.1
Triton	103	1.3	1.3	0.0

[a] Minority defined as African-American and Hispanic.

make no difference, but simply that the increasing foundation aid can dwarf the financial losses from choice and thereby weaken the influence of market mechanisms.

Table 4–5 shows the financial impact of choice for the largest net sending and receiving districts, which are the same as those listed in table 4–4. Considering sending districts first, we see that the absolute values of tuition payments for choice students are indeed large for these districts, ranging from a low of about $350,000 for Ayer to a high of about $955,000 for Springfield. But many of these districts also have very large enrollments, particularly those with higher poverty levels, and thus the effect of choice as a percentage of expenditures is quite small in these cases.

For example, the highest tuition payments are made by Springfield, which also has the highest poverty level (and the highest percent minority), and yet these tuition payments represent less than 1 percent of Springfield's total expenditures. A similar situation occurs for Brockton and Lynn, which both have high poverty and minority levels—the financial impact is only about 1 percent of total expenditures. It should be noted that these figures do not show reimbursements for foundation aid, which further reduce the financial impact of choice losses.

Significantly, the largest negative financial impact of choice occurs for the Triton (–3.1%), Gloucester (-3.2%), and Maynard (–5.5%) school districts, which have relatively low poverty levels and low to very low minority enrollments (see table 4–4). The reason for these larger effects is that these districts are quite small, with enrollments of less than 4,000, while the high-minority, high-poverty districts of Springfield, Brockton, and Lynn are large districts with enrollments of over 13,000. Therefore, the loss of 100 or more students for the smaller senders has a much larger relative impact on their total expenditures. In other words, the greatest adverse financial

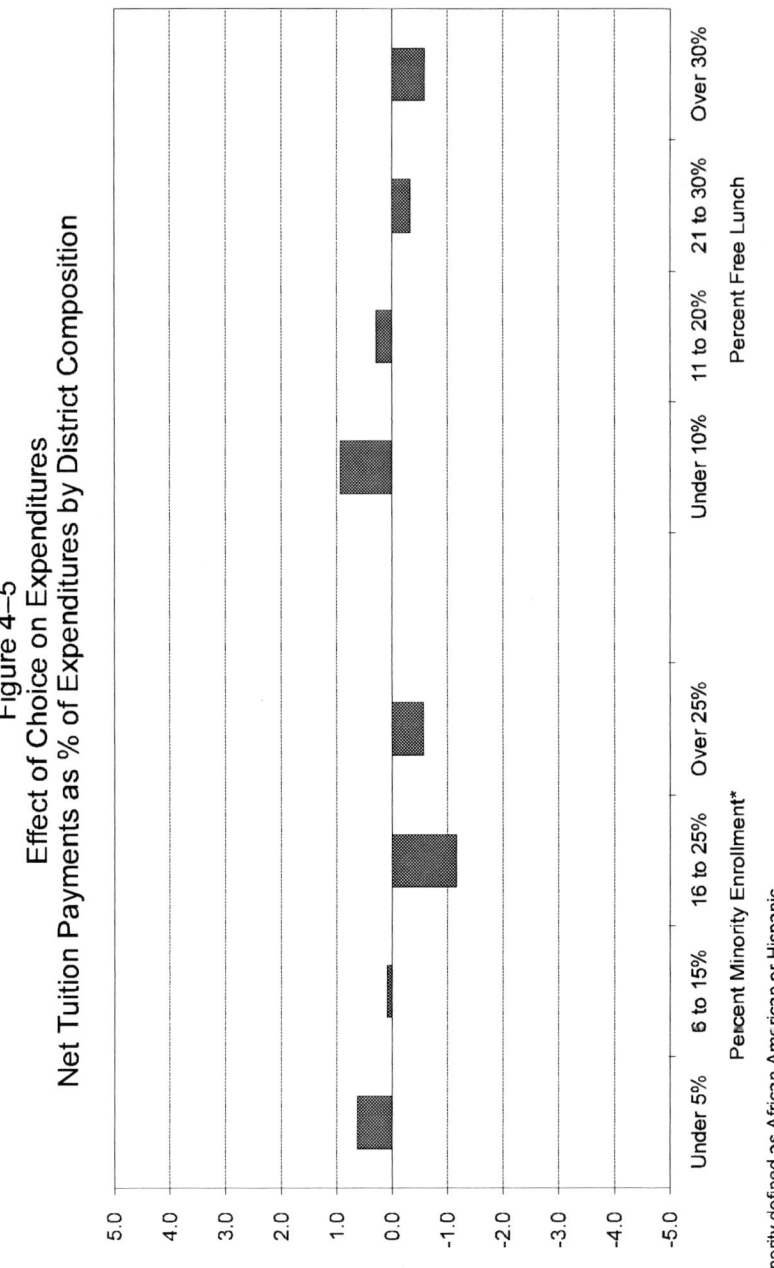

Figure 4–5
Effect of Choice on Expenditures
Net Tuition Payments as % of Expenditures by District Composition

Table 4-5
Financial Impact of Choice for Largest Senders and Receivers, 1994–95

District	Poverty Rate (%)	Tuition Received ($)	Tuition Paid ($)	Net Change As % of Expenditure
SENDERS WITH MORE THAN 100 CHOICE TRANSFERS OUT				
Springfield	69	0	954,914	−0.8
Triton	12	230,788	791,558	−3.1
Fitchburg	43	187,605	546,278	−1.6
Brockton	42	0	739,376	−1.1
Leominster	27	166,126	550,654	−1.7
Lynn	52	0	597,678	−1.0
Haverhill	29	44,202	498,148	−1.4
Lowell	60	0	441,188	−0.6
Gloucester	25	0	655,261	−3.2
Amesbury	17	238,978	426,479	−1.7
Maynard	13	111,220	533,955	−5.5
Milford	15	317,601	399,891	−0.5
Pittsfield	29	0	428,173	−1.2
Northbridge	21	216,696	372,838	−1.8
Salem	41	0	360,854	−1.4
Ayer	36	226,513	356,246	−1.5
Worcester	49	0	416,631	−0.4
RECEIVERS WITH MORE THAN 100 CHOICE TRANSFERS IN				
Holliston	3	1,105,374	33,168	8.1
Acton-Boxborough	1	1,223,078	60,926	9.4
Avon	10	895,849	0	20.6
Pentucket	7	630,793	152,802	3.3
Nashoba	6	824,723	317,482	3.1
Harvard	2	729,124	95,345	10.4
Newburyport	9	635,404	141,187	3.8
Hamilton-Wenham	4	726,130	49,756	6.2
Berkshire Hills	14	651,532	373,423	2.4
Marblehead	8	585,707	3,612	3.8
Manchester	5	667,796	25,346	13.7
Uxbridge	14	409,915	123,146	4.0
Lunenburg	7	325,516	121,084	2.8
Hampden-Wilbraham	8	479,887	7,314	2.2
Masconomet	2	463,335	27,050	5.3
Southwick-Tolland	17	360,762	32,670	3.7
Milford	15	317,601	399,891	−0.5
Triton	12	230,788	791,558	−3.1

effects do not occur for the school districts with the highest levels of minority and poverty enrollment.

The financial effects of choice on receiving districts with the largest choice enrollments are much greater, relative to expenditures, than on the sending districts. In the case of these receiving districts, not only are the absolute values of the tuition payments large—two districts exceed $1 million in tuition gains—but the relative impact on percentage gains are also very high. Avon, Harvard, and Manchester have realized gains of greater than 10 percent of total expenditures as a result of choice (Avon is highest at 20 percent), and many others have gained in the 5 to 9 percent range. Again, the reason for these large relative gains is that the typical receiving district is smaller than the typical sending district.

It appears from these data, then, that choice does not lead to significant negative effects on poorer, high minority sending districts, mainly because their enrollments—and corresponding budgets—are among the largest in the state. Indeed, negative financial effects are greatest in smaller sending districts that tend to have low proportions of minority and poverty students.

We will examine the financial impacts of choice over time in our 20 case study districts in chapter 5.

Conclusions

It is not uncommon in policy analysis to discover that reality is more complex than presumed by either critics or proponents of the policy in question. In the case of interdistrict choice as implemented in Massachusetts to date, we have found some evidence to support both sides of the debate. On the one hand, we find that receiving districts tend to be more affluent and less minority than sending districts on average, and also that interdistrict choice students tend to be more affluent, more academically skilled, and less minority than the average sending school population.

On the other hand, considerable choice is occurring among districts that are predominantly white, where race cannot be an issue, and there are a significant number of instances among the largest net sending districts in which choice students are actually academically less skilled than their respective resident populations. If we consider all net senders together, the differences in social and academic characteristics between senders and receivers is not as large as critics have argued.

Most important, we find very small effects of choice on the racial composition or the financial health of high minority, low wealth, sending districts, whether we consider all senders or just those with the largest choice losses. The reason for this finding is that the districts with the highest concentrations of minority and poor students also have large total enrollments. When the choice losses are expressed as percentages, the impact on racial composition is less than 1 percentage point and the impact on total expenditures is between .5 and 1.5 percent.

Choice actually raises the percent minority of net receiving districts to a somewhat greater degree than it lowers the percent minority in sending districts, although the effects are still very small. In this respect, it is important to note that the largest racial impact on a single district, in either a positive or negative direction, was on Avon: choice raised the percent minority by just over 1 percent in this predominately white receiving district.

Finally, it would be wrong to conclude that Massachusetts choice programs are not equitable for white and minority students. If we combine enrollment in all Massachusetts choice programs, including METCO and charter schools, we find good racial and ethnic representation, and in fact African-American students are actually overrepresented in choice programs in comparison to the total state population.

This leads us to conclude that the interdistrict choice program has a negative outcome in terms of representation, but because of small numbers of transfers relative to total enrollment, there is no significant adverse racial or financial impact on sending districts at this point. Of course, if the interdistrict choice program were to expand and there were larger numbers of transfers out from the high-minority districts, then this racial disparity could increase in the future.

At this point, however, we cannot evaluate the significance of the representation finding, because we do not know why white families take greater advantage of the choice program than minority families. It is important to determine the motivations of students and parents who change (or fail to change) school districts, and to investigate whether and to what extent choice families are motivated by racial rather than academic reasons. This question will be addressed in chapter 6.

CHAPTER FIVE

DOES MARKET COMPETITION IMPROVE SCHOOLS?

In the debate over school choice, perhaps no issue has been more contested than the applicability of "market" concepts for improving the quality of public education. Proponents of school choice believe that choice between public and nonpublic schools, funded by the state, would have a positive impact on public school quality. It would do so because parents and students, as consumers, would be more likely to choose effective schools over ineffective schools. Assuming that these choices would entail financial rewards or penalties for gaining or losing schools, as in the private sector, ineffective schools would be forced to either change their ways or shut their doors.

Opponents of choice reject the application of market concepts, claiming that schools, and particularly public school systems, are not analogous to business entities and cannot or will not respond to market pressures. These critics argue that choice—especially if it includes state-funded private and parochial schools—will simply cause middle-class students to leave lower SES public schools, leaving behind a harder-to-educate student body and less funds to do it. The losing districts would not be able to stop the losses, either because they have no funds to make improvements, or because race rather than programs is the real reason for the losses.

The same set of arguments applies to interdistrict public school choice. While interdistrict choice is more constrained than a full voucher system, in which students can choose from public or private schools, the market competition thesis can still apply as long as certain conditions are met, particularly that financial gains and losses result from the choice process. Public school districts that lose a significant number of students, so the argument goes, would simply have to improve quality in order to recover their losses. The opposing argument is also similar, that interdistrict choice will lead to a loss of middle-class students and funds from less advantaged districts, and that program improvements will be either impossible because of lack of funds or unworkable because they do not address the true reasons families are leaving.

The difficulty in applying market concepts to many statewide interdistrict choice plans is that the state provides most of the funding, so that districts that lose large numbers of students have little incentive (except pride) to win back market share. That is why the Massachusetts choice program is uniquely appropriate for testing the market competition thesis. Districts that send students must pay tuition to the districts that receive them out of their state aid money, and during the first two years of the Massachusetts program there were no reimbursement procedures for senders regardless of their financial status. Although low-wealth sending districts began getting substantial reimbursements in 1993, they still experience some financial loss because of the choice program.

This chapter aims to test the market competition thesis using data from 10 pairs of net receiving and sending districts in Massachusetts. Although we are also interested in the characteristics of the choice students and districts in this sample, the most important question here is the extent to which the choice law affected these districts in ways consistent or inconsistent with the market competition thesis.

APPROACH AND DATA FOR TESTING THE MARKET THESIS

A proper test of the market competition thesis requires some understanding of the dynamics of market processes, and particularly the fact that adverse market outcomes do not automatically translate into positive results for all enterprises. The market competition thesis must also be translated and given operational meaning in the context of public school systems.

When faced with new or increased competition in the market, an enterprise can respond in several ways. First, if the competition does not lead to any significant losses or adverse effects for a given enterprise, and it is satisfied with its market share, there is no reason for management to make any changes to its product or its way of doing business (response 1). Second, if new competition leads to serious losses in market share because people prefer the new product over the old, the management of the losing enterprise can institute corrective actions, such as heeding consumer views and improving its product, thereby recovering some or all of its losses (response 2).[1] Or it can fail to take corrective actions for whatever reason or make the wrong corrections (e.g., improve advertising instead of the product), and continue to lose market share (response 3).

Applying this model to public schools, a district that loses choice students can respond in these ways as well.[2] Just as in the business sector, we would expect some enterprises to fail for a variety of reasons, such as unwillingness to change or ineffective changes, and

---

[1] In some markets an enterprise may have a good product but consumers are not aware of it; we doubt this applies to public school systems who are losing resident students, because the local families should be quite familiar with the product.
[2] There may be other responses, such as "anti-competitive" responses in which agencies set out to undermine the market process, but we have no evidence of such actions in our sample.

therefore we would expect some school districts to fall into response 3. We would expect, however, that if the market competition thesis applies to public school districts, then more school districts should fall into response categories 1 and 2 than category 3.

What kinds of responses would we expect if the critics are right and market concepts do not apply to public school districts? First, most districts that lose a significant number of choice students should experience adverse effects, especially financial losses. Second, adversely affected districts should not be able to make effective changes and recover their losses, which means they should mostly fall into response category 3. In the case of public schools, this might happen for one of two reasons: (1) either they do not have enough funds to improve their programs, especially after paying tuition costs for the choice students, or (2) the cause of the losses is racial or socioeconomic composition, over which districts have no control.

We tested this operational definition of market competition using three sets of data. The first set was derived from school district site visits and was used to classify each sending district into one of the three types of responses: No Effect (response 1), Change (response 2), and No Change (response 3). The second two sets of data were used to validate this classification, and to verify whether real changes occurred in market share based on official data. In other words, we not only investigated whether school district management changed their programs or policies in response to loss of market share, but whether those changes were actually effective in restoring market share by either bringing students back or attracting new students in.

Although we believe the more critical test of the market thesis concerns the responses of school districts that lose market share, we must not ignore the response of districts that gain market share, the net receivers. If the market thesis applies, we expect net receivers to reap benefits from choice by improving or maintaining high-quality programs, thereby retaining their increased market share.

The first set of data came from staff interviews during our site visits at the 10 pairs of sending and receiving districts. We asked both structured and unstructured questions about specific effects of the choice law on their district's policies and programs. The structured questions asked about positive or negative effects of choice on the number of teachers, number of support staff, number or type of courses, supplies and equipment, extracurricular activities, class sizes, and maintenance or renovation activities. Unstructured (open-end) questions asked for detailed information about specific impacts on programs and resources, why choice students leave or enter their district, and opinions about the choice law including recommendations for changes. For sending districts we focused on whether the choice losses were perceived as a problem, whether the losses led to changes in their policies and programs, and what types of changes were made (see appendix B for interview schedule).

In most districts we interviewed 3 or 4 school staff members, typically the superintendent, a school committee member, and one or two principals; occasionally we interviewed an assistant superintendent or a business manager. Altogether we interviewed 69 staff or school committee members in 19 districts, including 18 superintendents, 14 school committee members, 13 high school principals, 8 middle/junior high school principals, and 7 elementary school principals.

The second set of state data includes total receiving and sending student counts, tuition transfer payments, and total expenditures. This information was tabulated for the time period 1992–93 to 1995–96, so that we could examine trends over time in both enrollment and tuition payments. By examining the data for groups of sending school districts classified according to the three market responses, we were able to test the validity of the classification. We were also able to test whether the sending districts who made changes in programs in response to choice losses (Change) were effective in stopping or reversing loss in market share.

The state data on expenditures are also used to evaluate the effects of the choice law on trends in per pupil expenditures. Although all sending districts pay tuition to receivers, a complex reimbursement formula alleviates some of the costs of choice losses, and this formula is more beneficial to low-wealth senders than to other senders. When combined with the foundation aid to low-wealth school districts, the financial burden of choice losses is reduced. Thus we need to examine trends in total school expenditures in order to assess the ultimate financial impacts of choice as mediated by state funding mechanisms.

Finally, the third set of data attempts to replicate the results from the original 10 sending districts with a second set of sending districts that had not received site visits. Specifically, we examined enrollment trends for all other sending districts that had 100 or more choice transfers out in 1994–95 to see if loss patterns replicated the findings in our case study sample.

IMPACT OF CHOICE ON SENDING DISTRICT PROGRAMS

The staff interviews at the sending districts revealed considerable variation from one district to another in the responses to choice losses. These variations were consistent with three types of responses about the perceived severity of the initial choice losses and about how the district responded to their choice losses. Two of these patterns corresponded rather closely to the "No Effect" and "Change" categories. The third type of response corresponded approximately to the "No Change" category, although there was less agreement among staff in the third group of districts either about the seriousness of the losses or whether any changes had been initiated. Generally, there was considerable consensus among staff opinions in both the No Effect and the Change districts.

We will first summarize the interview results for each response type, followed by illustrative quotes from the open-end questions on choice impacts. We then summarize some of the closed-end questions on choice impacts as a partial check on the internal consistency of responses.

THE NO EFFECT DISTRICTS

The staff interviews at three sending districts corresponded strongly and consistently with the No Effect category. The staff at these districts perceived few adverse effects on programs and resources resulting from the loss of choice students. While they were not happy about the loss of students, they indicated that there had been no negative effect on programs such as laying off teachers, dropping or changing courses or activities, or reducing operational expenses. Indeed, most of these staff members saw no problems with the quality of their programs, and believed the real reasons for choice losses were related either to misperceptions about the quality of their academic programs or to racial motivations. Consequently, staff in these districts reported no major changes in policies or programs designed to stop or slow down the losses.

We do not mean that the staff was unconcerned about the impact of choice losses; at least one staff member in every district (and several in one district) complained about the adverse impact on diversity, since the choice students were disproportionately white compared to the students left behind. Since table 4–4 shows virtually no impact of choice losses on racial composition for any sending district in our sample, however, it is more likely that these staff members were referring to their perceptions of why students leave rather than the actual impact on racial composition. In fact, in response to a question about why students leave, over 60 percent of the staff in these districts indicated that choice students were primarily motivated by racial/ethnic considerations; the second most common reason mentioned was safety. See chapter 6 for the reasons for changing districts given by parents, students, and receiving district staff.

The only concrete changes to programs or policies mentioned were improved public relations programs, and, in one case, accelerating the decision to become a receiving district. There was a general feeling that the quality of their programs was good, or at least as good as that of the receiving schools, and that the main problem was one of perception of quality, not the reality of quality. This view was reinforced by the majority view that the primary reason students left was racial in nature, which was a condition over which they had no control. Only one staff member in one of these three districts mentioned a concrete change involving some curriculum and scheduling improvements.

Some direct quotes from the staff interviews illustrate why these districts are classified into the No Effect category:

> [We need] better publicity. You know, more positive programs in the paper. Of course, positive programs don't sell. I mean, [District] has some excellent programs going on...[Is there anything that you're doing differently?] Not in response. The numbers we've lost have not been noticeable and really we offer what I consider a very good program...Number one reason that parents go for choice has nothing to do with dissatisfaction about their child's education...The number one reason was racial issues and perception.

> [Reason students leave?] We conducted a survey...[one] reason was geographic location...[school in other district]

was closer...Another reason is overall size of the student body [other districts smaller]...and another is... some racial things that were indicated...Academic superiority or excellence was not mention one single time. [Did it have any specific impact on polices or programs?] No. The only impact it had was loss of state aid...There were no teachers that were pink slipped because there was a decline in enrollment...It didn't have an impact in terms of our changing our policy or programs...it may have had an impact in terms of purchasing supplies...but it didn't impact the course that we were offering...It probably had us look more carefully at choice, whether or not we should [become a receiver]...I think it may have accelerated the [school] decision to go with choice.

Whenever something good at the school goes on we make a conscious effort to publicize it...We began sending out a newsletter to parents...[Reason students leave?] Right now one is absolutely racial...[Impact of losses?] It has skimmed off some of what are the best and brightest. No [loss of programs]; because we are such a large district, I don't think we've lost anything, really...But now we're little more pro-active about our schools, about what's going on in our schools.

[Reasons students leave?] One is, outright, people don't want to be in integrated schools...Second, an increasing perception of violence in the community and in the schools...It's a perception, it's not based on reality...We do have a very organized violence prevention program...The third thing is that the quality of the schools are not as good as [other districts]...In some cases it's true, and in some cases it's perception. And we're working to make it untrue everywhere...[Impact of losses?] They negatively impact...you can't ask me to integrate the schools, and then let...white kids go to [other districts] that are mostly white. [Any specific impacts?] I like to think not, but many of the kids who leave are very good students...I wouldn't give them the satisfaction of [changing programs].

[Reason students leave?] In my opinion, I think I would have to say that perhaps the reason might be racially motivated... When I have asked, is there a problem with the curriculum or the teacher, it's none of that. I can't think of another reason. [Impact of losses?] The only impact that I would be able to note would be a dwindling white population...I don't think we have done anything [to programs]. I think we feel as if we have a good program in place.

A total of 11 staff were interviewed in these three No Effect districts, and they each rated the possible effects of choice on the seven specific program areas listed above. Of the 77 total responses, 71 (92 percent) were "No Effect." Three staff indicated reductions in class size (usually not seen as a negative effect), one an increase in class size, one an increase in support staff, and one a decrease in support staff.

As further validation of the No Effect classification, all of these districts had voted against becoming receiving districts as of the 1995–96 school year, although one was planning to start in the fall of 1996. Becoming a receiving district is the easiest way to reduce lost revenues, assuming that some number of students can be attracted to that district.

THE CHANGE DISTRICTS

Staff at three other sending districts provided information consistent with the Change response. The majority of these staff stated that the loss of choice students had serious—if not devastating—effects on the quality of their school programs and resources. They said, further, that after recovering from the initial shock, the school system and the community had responded aggressively to this negative impact by making significant changes in school programs and funding. Staff in more than one district described the choice losses as a "wake up call." In some cases the improvements simply restored lost resources, and in other cases the improvements actually increased resources beyond the levels before the choice policy. Unexpectedly, because the ultimate result of these initial adverse effects was significant improvement in programs, their overall view of the choice law was both positive and supportive in spite of their initial losses of students and resources.

Quotes from staff interviews illustrate the initially adverse but ultimately positive impact of choice at these three sending districts:

> Let me cite the positive part first. I think the fact that a lot of kids left and continue to stay out had the effect of being an academic wake-up call to our faculty, because no longer could they automatically count on having a student go through our schools just because they lived in town...The two negatives are ...when you lose 10 percent of a [grade]...that may be the critical mass that causes you to not be able to offer a course...or you have to discontinue a sports team...The most negative piece is the financial piece...we lose [in tuition payments] more than three times what the state would have paid us if the kid had stayed here...[What happened after the wake-up call?] In the three years that we've gone in for school budget increases...I've been able to get a school increase [from the town] of 6 percent each year...when we went to the Finance Committee...and said to them, 'We've got to do this in order to bring our school academically up to snuff,' they said, 'Fine, we want to support that.'

> [It] has resulted in our having a more stable budget. It's resulted in our being able to put back programs that we lost because of a declining budget and a lack of support in the town.

> It's a bad news-good news story. Because it was the bad news that caused the good news...The town fathers and the finance

committee have increase our budget which was...$6.1 million in FY 93. Four years later, which will include next year's budget, it will be $9.8 million.[3]

We now offer full-day, part-day, and two-year kindergarten...Technology...now we have a technology guru on staff who spends $100,000 to $200,000 a year putting technology in certain locations. It's been a big change, a big increase.

So a big thing was to improve the main outlook on the schools—clean the windows, get the place clean, get the sander out. The Department of Public Works was great, they cleaned up the whole area. So what happened is the town's people come and, 'wow, look at the difference'...and then I started getting phone calls.

[Initially] some people felt betrayed...there was a lot of anger and disenchantment because...most of the ones who left weren't long-time residents...didn't have loyalty...[We had] a conference, it was 'Save [District] Schools'...where we had key stakeholders who got off site for a couple of days with a good facilitator and identified a vision statement, mission statement...One of the common visions was a first-rate educational system, a first rate educational plant...The last three years we've averaged 11 percent increases in the operating budget...And then the capital expenditure, an elementary school [had] a $7 million rehab and addition...[and] a $9 million rehab and addition to the middle-high school. So there has been a renaissance, a reawakening, a revitalization.[4]

---

[3] Later in the interview, the respondent indicated that some of this money (unspecified) was due to the state's foundation budget program.
[4] This respondent also identified foundation aid as a contributor to the turnaround, as well as the choice losses.

Part of it I think would be...commitment. Not that there wasn't a commitment before but just that school choice, as we all call it, [was] a wake-up call. The commitment, the technology is incredible...The old timers are willing to jump on board. They're learning computers. They have PCs in their classrooms...The sports teams started winning Super Bowls and...state championships...And I'll tell you the staff never changed. But mentally they were up. It was a morale builder...The best thing...was the senior class of '93. Those kids were unbelievable; they came to forums; they talked to people; they formed a group, SOS, Save Our Schools...They came to the School Committee...They went to Selectmen's meetings, and they talked about how much they loved [District], and how did they let people go to other school systems, 'Please support our staff, and us, we'll do anything you want.' It was unbelievable.

The year before choice went into effect...we had cut our budget...I had 39 teachers and 13 were either eliminated or reduced in time...The [choice] bill passed and all of a sudden within 3 or 4 days we had a massive exodus...Probably the best thing that ever happened to the town. What happened since them is that first of all the budget has been adequately funded. Secondly, it created a great deal of pride in the people...The senior class had lost a lot of kids...The Valedictorian got up at graduation, and she talked about all the accomplishments...Then she finished the thing up and she said, 'For all of you people that pulled your kids out of the town, and all of you people who lost faith in us, I give you the class of 1993!'...the whole place went wild. It was a very emotional speech...and I think her speech...may have turned the tide...Then the whole town got in on it...and the people that were voting against increases in the budget, all of a sudden saw that their property values were going down. We were having trouble getting money...to renovate a school...Went to the Town Meeting and I think the vote was

500 to 3 to fund the thing for $12 million. So it totally turned people's minds...

Of the 12 staff interviewed in these three districts, 10 believed that the ultimate effects of choice were positive in that they led to increased resources and/or enhancements in specific program areas, especially the number of teachers and course offerings. One respondent believed that choice ultimately allowed maintenance of programs, and only one respondent indicated there were no overall positive or negative effects of choice.

THE NO CHANGE DISTRICTS

The remaining three districts are classified as No Change districts, primarily on the basis of staff reports that indicated there were few specific program or policy improvements aimed at reducing choice losses. There was less consensus on the severity of adverse effects arising because of choice losses, although adverse program effects were claimed by at least one staff member in each district. At least one staff member in two of these districts mentioned improvement in public relations efforts, because they believed choice losses were caused by misperceptions of district programs. Since the staff at these districts have somewhat different response patterns and less consensus about adverse effects, we will describe each district separately.

In one of these districts the superintendent said there were no specific negative impacts on programs or resources, but the business manager said there were adverse impacts on a number of program areas resulting in reductions in teachers, support staff, and supplies/equipment. None of the staff reported improvements to programs and resources in order to recover choice losses, with the exception of improvements to their public relations programs and the development of brochures.

Does Market Competition Improve Schools? 91

Another district had a similar pattern of responses, but in this case the superintendent reported adverse effects in several areas including reductions of teachers, support staff, supplies and equipment, and extracurricular activities. This respondent also mentioned a negative impact from losing middle-class students. Another staff member mentioned reductions in course offerings, especially honors sections, and also general loss of funds. In this district, neither staff member mentioned specific program or policy improvements at that time, although one respondent said they were in the process of doing a survey and studying possible areas for improvement.

Finally, in a third district the majority of staff agreed that choice had caused serious adverse effects in many program areas such as reductions of teachers, loss of courses, reduced supply and equipment budgets, increased class sizes, and reduced maintenance budgets. Two of the three staff members here said there had been no significant program changes in response to choice losses, although both indicated there had been some program improvements unrelated to choice losses. Another staff member said that choice losses had been a factor in (but not the sole cause of) facility improvement, particularly a new high school that was under construction. There is some evidence here of changes due to choice, but the lack of consensus leads us to leave it in the No Change category.

IMPACT OF CHOICE ON RECEIVING DISTRICT PROGRAMS

In contrast to the sending districts, there was very little variation among the staff at net receiving districts about the impact of the choice law, with large majorities reporting positive effects in a number of specific program and resource areas. The positive responses were generally consistent across both closed- and open-end questions.

In the closed-end questions, for example, almost 90 percent of receiving district staff said that choice funds led either to increases in or maintenance of the number of teachers, where maintenance means they would have lost teachers in the absence of choice funds (61 and 28%, respectively). Almost 70 percent indicated additions or maintenance of specific courses, in some cases restoring courses that had been cut earlier due to budget constraints (22 and 47%). About 63 percent also indicated increases in or maintenance of supplies and equipment expenditures. Positive impacts were reported less frequently in the area of facility upkeep and renovation efforts (improvements 33%, upkeep 17%) and in the area of extra-curricular activities (additions 11%, maintenance 39%).

One effect usually viewed as negative was increased class sizes, which was reported by 42 percent of receiving district staff; only 19 percent reported reduced class sizes. It must be noted, however, that before choice many of these school districts had very low enrollments, even declining enrollments, and some had class sizes that were too small. Thus in some of these districts an increase in class size was actually perceived as a benefit, allowing them to maintain courses that might otherwise have been dropped.

The open-end questions were generally consistent with this picture, with a few variations. Increases or maintenance of faculty and courses received the highest number of mentions, with courses slightly ahead of faculty (40 percent to 34 percent). Supplies and equipment mentions were tied with class sizes at 29 percent. Another frequently mentioned item not included in the fixed-response items was the type of student coming into the district. Nearly 30 percent of the receiving staff mentioned this as important, in terms of either the diversity, academic quality, or commitment of the choice students.

From the market competition point of view, it is significant that a number of the net receiving districts were having problems sustaining their academic programs before choice, mainly due to small (and shrinking) enrollments. In these cases the choice law actually strengthened their programs and made them more competitive.

VALIDATION OF RESPONSES

The interview data provide considerable evidence that school districts have responded to choice losses in ways consistent with the market competition thesis. The ultimate test of whether the model applies, however, is not merely whether challenged enterprises make changes or attempt to make changes in their product, but whether these changes are actually effective in restoring or at least reversing loss of market share.

This final test must be conducted using direct measures of changes in market share, which in this case are trends in choice enrollments and tuition payments. Enrollment and tuition data will also help test the validity of our classification of sending districts into the three response categories.

The analysis of market responses is based on only 10 net sending districts, which is a very small number compared to the number of sending districts in Massachusetts (although it includes a high proportion of districts with large choice losses). Thus we will attempt to replicate our findings using enrollment data from all other sending districts who lost 100 or more choice students in 1994–95.

The central question here is whether the program improvements in the Change districts were effective in actually reversing the trends in choice enrollment, either by reducing transfers out or by increasing transfers in. In addition, we would not expect such reversals in the No Change and the No Effects groups, since they have not taken special steps to improve their programs in response to choice. We would expect, however, if our interview data are reliable, that both the Change and the No Change groups would reveal greater initial adverse effects from enrollment and tuition losses than the No Effect group.

RESULTS FOR CASE STUDY DISTRICTS

Using state reports on the number of choice students transferring out of sending districts and enrolling in receiving districts, we computed the net choice enrollments for all 20 districts in our target sample for each year between FY1993 and FY1996.[5] The net choice enrollment for a district is the number of choice students entering (if any) minus the number of choice students leaving (if any). We also computed the net tuition payments in the same way, tuition received minus tuition paid out. We expressed these net choice enrollments and tuition payments as absolute numbers as well as percentages based on total enrollment and total expenditures.

Table 5–1 presents the trends in net choice enrollment and net tuition payments for the 10 sending districts in our sample classified by response category.[6] The choice enrollment and tuition payment trends are quite consistent with our classification of districts, and most importantly they support a conclusion that the program improvements made by the Change group were indeed effective.

All three districts in the Change group show significant reductions in net losses from the year of their maximum net loss. District 3 has had the greatest degree of success, actually changing from a net sending district in 1994 to a net receiving district in 1996. The other

---

[5] Data by district were available only for the last four years of the choice program. See appendix A for the raw numbers used for our calculations.
[6] The sending district that did not participate in our site visits is shown as District 10.

Table 5-1
Trends in Choice Enrollment and Tuition Payments for Sending Districts

Sender	1992–93	1993–94	1994–95	1995–96	Percent Reduction[a]
NET CHANGE IN ENROLLMENT					
CHANGE GROUP					
District 1	–100	–81	–62	–51	49
District 2	–103	–126	–102	–76	40
District 3	–43	–91	–26	+12	100
NO CHANGE GROUP					
District 4	–141	–139	–145	–129	11
District 5	–1	–58	–121	–146	0
District 6	–81	–137	–106	–122	11
NO EFFECT GROUP					
District 7	–78	–151	–128	–114	25
District 8	–59	–74	–154	–147	5
District 9	–158	–284	–258	–292	0
District 10	–141	–166	–188	–190	0
TUITION LOSSES, $000					
CHANGE GROUP					
District 1	–343	–247	–219	–196	43
District 2	–417	–542	–423	–378	30
District 3	–156	–255	–156	–110	57
NO CHANGE GROUP					
District 4	–655	–567	–655	–568	13
District 5	–42	–179	–359	–506	0
District 6	–283	–434	–385	–449	0
NO EFFECT GROUP					
District 7	–255	–475	–454	–422	11
District 8	–244	–286	–598	–652	0
District 9	–480	–976	–955	–1,118	0
District 10	–566	–699	–739	–831	0

[a] From year of largest net loss to 1995–96.

two districts in the Change group also show positive trends, one showing a 49 percent reduction in net losses and one showing a 40 percent reduction.

These reductions were caused by a combination of reduced transfers out and increased transfers in. For example, between 1994 and 1996 District 3 reduced transfers out by 47 and increased transfers in by 52; District 2 reduced transfers out by 24 and increased transfers in by 14 during the same time period; and between 1993 and 1996 District 1 reduced transfers out by 33 and increased transfers in by 6 (see appendix A and figure 5–1).

The No Change group shows one district with no reductions in net loss and two districts (4 and 6) with reductions in net losses of 11 percent. District 4 is not a receiving school, so all of the reduction comes from 16 fewer transfers out between 1995 and 1996. This happens to be the district where staff disagreed about whether choice losses had contributed to facility improvement.[7] The other district with a small reduction in transfers out, District 6, voted to become a receiver starting in 1994–95 and had 65 transfers in the first year and 79 the second year; the transfers out continued to increase all four years. The reduction was the result of a decision to become a receiving school, which by definition means the choice law was the causal agent. In any event, neither of these reductions approach the magnitude documented for the Change group.

Finally, one district in the No Effect group shows no reduction in net choice losses, one district shows an insignificant reduction of 5 percent, and District 7 shows a reduction of 25 percent. All of the reduction in net losses in District 7 came from a decision to become a receiver in 1994–95, and it gained 26 students in that year and 45 the

---

[7] District 4 became a receiver for the first time in the 1996–97 school year.

next year; transfers out remained steady during the last three years. This is the only district in the No Effect group that was a receiver during these four years; this is the district in which one staff member said that choice losses had accelerated a decision to become a receiving district.[8] Finally, the main receiving district for District 7 has stopped choice transfers at certain grade levels due to capacity constraints, which may be responsible for the leveling off of transfers out. It appears, then, that the one significant reduction in choice losses for the No Effect group is not improvement in school programs but rather a decision to take advantage of the choice law, coupled with reduced opportunities for choice students to transfer out.

The trends in tuition losses, shown in the lower portion of table 5–1, are generally consistent with the trends in enrollment losses. All districts in the change group have experienced substantial reductions in net tuition payments. The percentage reductions in tuition payments are generally smaller than for enrollment losses, probably because the tuition paid for transfers out are higher than for transfers in (per pupil expenditures for receiving districts are generally higher than those for sending districts, see figure 5–4). Only two districts in the No Change and No Effect group show reductions in tuition losses from their peak loss year, and neither approach the magnitude of reduction shown for the Change districts.

It is worth noting that District 10, which did not participate in the site visits, is not a receiving district and therefore all its net losses are due to transfers out. Although we have no interview data with which to classify this district, it would not be surprising if it fell into the No Effect category.

---

[8] District 9 became a receiver for the first time in the 1996–97 school year.

We also examined the trends in relative changes in choice enrollment and tuition payments, that is, losses and gains expressed as percentages of total enrollment or total expenditures. We want to confirm that the trends in relative effects are consistent with absolute effects, and to see if our classification of adverse effects is consistent with choice impacts when we measure them relative to total district enrollment and expenditures. This relative change analysis also includes the trends for all receiving districts.

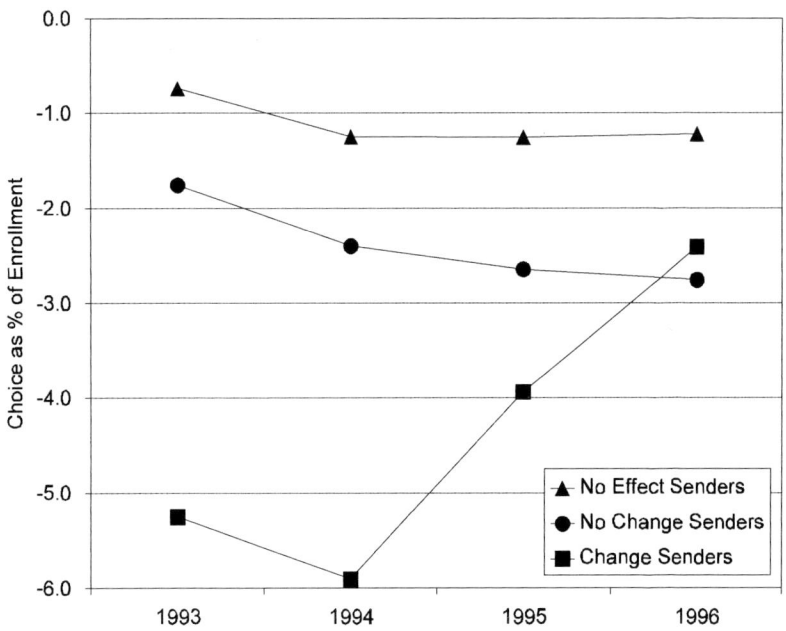

Figure 5-1
Trends in Choice Enrollment
Case Study Senders

Figure 5-1 shows average trends in choice enrollment as a percentage of total enrollment for each group of districts. We see that of the three sending district groups, the No Effect group shows the smallest relative losses, and the Change group shows the largest relative losses. In the 1993–94 school year, for example, choice losses averaged 6 percent of total enrollment for the Change group and only 1.2 percent of total enrollment for the No Effect group, a five-fold difference in magnitude. The No Change group is in the middle, as might be expected; losses averaged 2.4 percent of total enrollment, which is lower than the Change group, but twice the magnitude of the No Effect group. Moreover, over the next two years the No Change group experienced an increase in relative losses, to 2.8 percent, while the Change group reduced its relative losses to only 2.5 percent, cutting 1994 losses by more than half. The relative losses for the No Effect group are small and have little variation over the four-year period. This analysis clearly supports both our classification of sending districts as well as the effectiveness of program improvements made by the Change group.

Finally, we see that the relative gains in enrollment made by the average receiving group are much larger than the relative losses of any of the sending groups. They average about 10 percent in 1992–93 and rise to a high of about 13 percent in 1994–95. The reason for the larger relative effects for receivers than senders is that the average receiving district in this sample (and statewide) has a much smaller enrollment than the average sending district, particularly the senders in the No Effect group (see table 3–2).

Figure 5–2 shows the trends in tuition gains or losses expressed as a percentage of total district expenditures. The patterns of relative financial impact are very similar to the relative enrollment impacts shown in figure 5–1. The No Effect senders experience a financial loss of 1 percent or less due to choice tuition payments, while the Change senders experienced the greatest financial effects, especially in the 1993 and 1994 fiscal years. The No Change senders fall in between, but again the reduction in net choice losses for the Change group reduces their impact to about the same level as the No Change group in 1996. The tuition income for receiving districts has averaged somewhat over 8 percent of total expenditures for the past several years, which is less than their relative enrollment gain. This is consistent with the tuition cap of 75 percent that was placed on receiving district tuition in 1993.

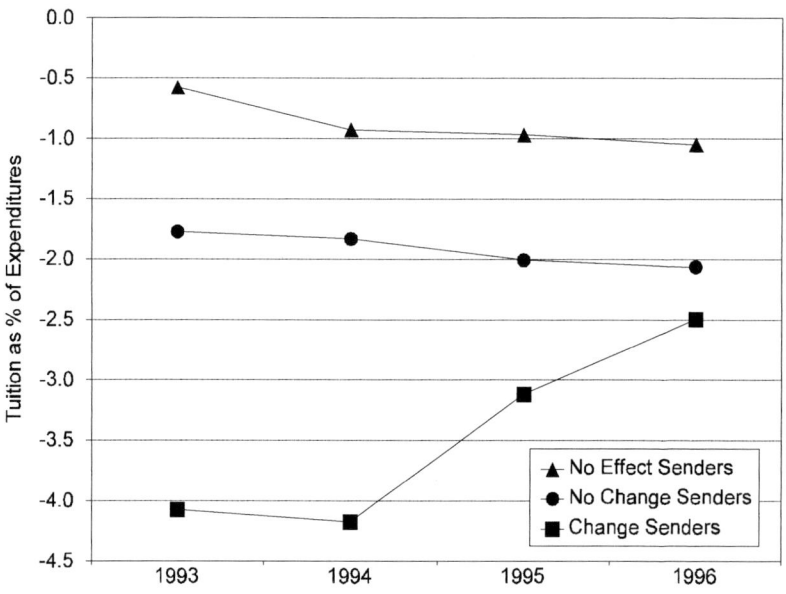

Figure 5-2
Trends in Tuition Gains/Losses
Case Study Senders

It should be noted that the relative effects for District 10 resembled those for the No Effect group, with choice losses of less than 2 percent of total enrollment and financial losses of about 1 percent of total expenditures. These data are consistent with District 10 being included in the No Effect group.

The trends in enrollment and tuition payments offer substantial validation of the classification of districts based on the district staff interviews. Choice losses in the No Effect districts indeed generate very small relative impacts on both enrollment and finances, and nearly all of the staff in these districts agreed that there were no significant adverse effects of choice losses. The enrollment and financial losses for the Change districts are much larger, and most of staff in these districts said the initial effects were extremely adverse. The fact that the No Change districts fall in between is evidence that the losses were not as severe for this group, one possible reason for the lack of clear attempts to improve their programs.

Most important, however, the enrollment and tuition trends show that the Change districts actually reversed their losses, which not only validates staff reports that they improved their programs but also demonstrates that program improvements were effective in restoring at least part of their lost market share. These districts have learned, firsthand, that market competition can be an impetus for school reforms that improve the quality of education programs.

CHOICE TRENDS IN OTHER LARGE SENDERS

Since the support for the market thesis found in our case study districts is based on only 10 sending districts, we must be cautious about generalizing from these results. In order to have some test of robustness for these findings, we examined enrollment trends in the remaining large net sending districts with 100 or more choice transfers out in the 1994–95 school year. Those nine districts were listed in table 3-3.

Since no site visits were made to these districts, we have no information about whether any of these districts actually made changes in their programs in response to choice losses. The analysis of case study districts, however, found a relationship between choice losses as a percentage of total enrollment (relative losses) and perception of serious adverse effects. All of the Change districts, who reported the most severe impacts, experienced relative choice losses of more than 4 percent of total enrollment in their worst year, while all of the No Effect districts experienced worst-year effects of less than 2 percent of total enrollment. The No Change districts had worst-year relative losses between 2 and 3 percent, and each of these districts had at least one staff member who perceived adverse effects of choice. There appears to be a threshold around 2 percent for the perception of serious adverse effects of choice losses.

Table 5–2 shows trends in net losses for the remaining nine large senders in Massachusetts, classified according to whether relative choice losses exceeded or were less than 2 percent of total enrollment in their worst year (see appendix A). In every case the high-loss districts show significant reductions in choice losses, with Ayer and Clinton revealing the largest reductions in losses.

The four districts that lost less than 2 percent of enrollment to choice show virtually no indication of reversing the trend of net losses, and net losses are still growing in three of the four districts. It should be noted that Milford is the only district in the low-impact group that is also a receiver; none of the other districts have tried to reduce their losses by voting to become a receiving district.

Among the high-impact districts, all but Salem have become receiving districts, which has clearly aided in reducing their net losses. For example, Ayer shows increased transfers in from 8 in 1993 to 111 in 1996, and Clinton transfers in have increased from 0 in 1993 to 62 in 1996. Amesbury has also increased transfers in from 43 to 118 (see appendix A).

Table 5-2
Trends in Choice Enrollment for Other Sending Districts with 100 or More Choice Transfers Out

District	1993	1994	1995	1996	Percent Reduction[a]
SENDER NET LOSS >2% OF ENROLLMENT					
Amesbury	26	−63	−59	−44	30
Ayer	−100	−87	−32	−15	85
Clinton	−23	−41	−62	−32	48
Salem	−24	−56	−104	−80	23
Triton	N/A	−67	−116	−96	17
SENDER NET LOSS <2% OF ENROLLMENT					
Lowell	−56	−142	−152	−160	0
Milford	6	−22	−15	−41	0
Pittsfield	−46	−72	−113	−111	2
Worcester	−59	−93	−109	−137	0

[a] From year of largest net loss.

A summary of the relative losses in these two groups of districts is shown in figure 5–3. The low-impact districts show overall lower relative losses and a trend of increasing losses relative to their total enrollment. The high-impact districts reached a maximum negative impact in 1995 but reduced that impact by about one-third in 1996. These data offer further support for the findings of the case study, that market forces appear to be at work in school districts as a result of the choice law.

IMPACT ON PER PUPIL EXPENDITURES

To this point we have tested the financial impact of market competition in terms of tuition gains and losses, either in absolute dollars or relative to total expenditures. While this information is important for determining whether districts behave according to market principles, it does not provide the entire story regarding financial incentives. We must also consider the impact of total district expenditures, particularly because, since 1993, Massachusetts has provided extra funds for districts whose spending was below foundation level.

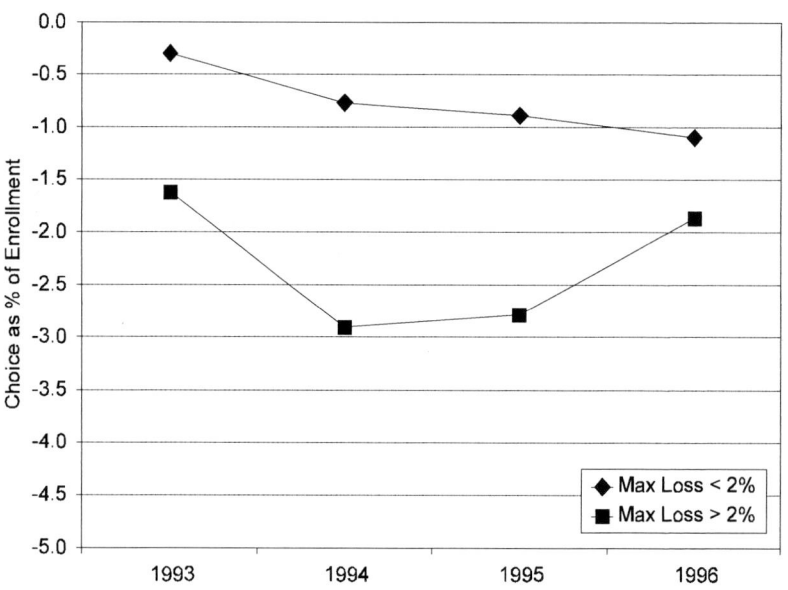

Figure 5-3
Trends in Choice Enrollment
Other Senders with 100+ Choice Out in 1995

The minimum per pupil expenditure required for an adequate education was termed the "foundation level" in the Education Reform Act of 1993. While the primary aim of the act is to equalize financing of public schools, its funding mechanisms also affect the choice policy. Basically, the law provides that a district with spending below foundation level will receive incremental aid each year, over a seven-year period, until it reaches the foundation level. The average foundation level was initially set at about $5,500, but it grows each year in response to inflation; it was nearly $5,800 in fiscal year 1995. The new foundation aid each year can be as much as $300 to $400 per student for low-wealth districts.

Foundation aid affects the financial impact of the choice program by altering market dynamics. Many of the sending districts with the most transfers out are below foundation, which means that they are receiving higher amounts of foundation aid each year, in addition to reimbursements for choice losses. For some of these districts, the financial impact of interdistrict choice losses is reduced by gains in foundation aid. Sending districts that are above foundation *and* have large numbers of transfers out may actually see their state aid go down from one year to the next.

Of our 10 sending districts, two were above foundation in 1994 and 1995 and another was at foundation in 1994 and slightly below in 1995. Both of the above foundation districts are in the Change group, and the borderline district is in the No Change group (District 4). All three No Effect districts are below foundation, as are two of the No Change districts. The two Change districts that are above foundation receive no foundation aid, but they received reimbursement for 50 percent of net tuition losses in the 1993 fiscal year and for 25 percent of net tuition losses in subsequent years. Thus, while their losses after 1993 are partially reimbursed, they do not receive any extra state aid because of their economic status.

The three No Effect and the two No Change districts that are below foundation receive a significant amount of state aid each year to bring them up to foundation levels; the increase can be on the order of 10 percent of a district's total budget each year. In 1994 they also received 100 percent of their 1993 choice tuition losses. In subsequent years they received 100 percent of any annual *increase* in choice tuition losses. Thus not only do these districts receive some reimbursements for tuition losses, they also receive large amounts of foundation aid.

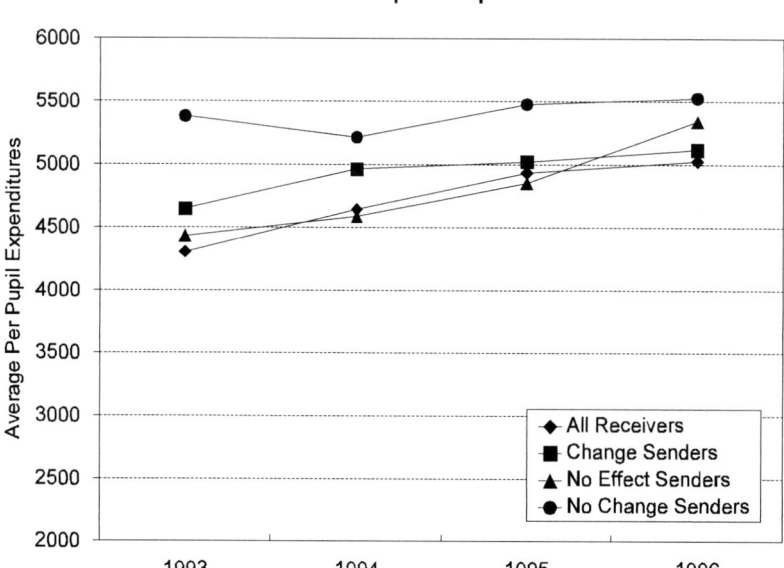

Figure 5-4
Trends in Per Capita Expenditures

Figure 5–4 shows the trends in per capita expenditures for all receivers and the three groups of senders in our sample between fiscal years 1993 and 1996. While the receiving districts have higher per capita funding than the sending districts, they show virtually no increase in per pupil expenditures during this period in spite of substantial gains in choice tuition income (these figures are not corrected for inflation). Since most receivers are above foundation, they are not receiving any increases in state aid, and therefore it appears that their tuition gains from choice are simply absorbed by the increased number of choice students they have to educate.

More striking, however, is that *all* groups of sending districts show substantial gains in per pupil expenditures regardless of category. In fact, the No Effect districts experienced the largest absolute gains in per capita expenditures, and they reduced the gap with receiving districts from $1,000 to $200 in spite of choice losses. Likewise, the No Change group shows increased funding in spite of choice losses. The Change group has also experienced increased expenditures, but at a lower rate than for the other two groups of senders, mainly because two out of the three Change districts are above foundation. As a result, the per pupil expenditure gap between receivers and senders was reduced markedly by 1996.

The tuition payments made by below foundation sending districts for transfers out, then, are more than made up for by foundation aid. While these sending districts end up with less than they would have had without choice losses, the foundation aid and tuition reimbursements may ameliorate market incentives and penalties.

IMPLICATIONS FOR THE MARKET THESIS

The evidence presented here strongly supports the notion that market concepts can be applied to public schools and that some school districts will improve school quality in response to market competition. There are several ways in which our findings are consistent with the market thesis and inconsistent with the arguments of critics who reject the application of market concepts to public schools.

First, the behavior of three of the nine sending districts conform to a classic market response: they lost a substantial fraction of their enrollment, the leadership correctly perceived an adverse impact from the loss of students, they responded by changing their policies and programs, and they became more aggressive about promoting their improved programs. Most important, all of them demonstrated the effectiveness of the improvements by significantly reducing their net choice losses, in one case by actually becoming a net receiver.

Second, three additional sending districts conform to another legitimate market response: they lost a small fraction of their enrollment, they did not experience significant adverse effects on resources and programs (according to both staff reports and financial data), and consequently they had no reason to change their programs in order to stop the losses. A fourth sending district not visited fits the No Effect profile according to the enrollment and financial data.

Third, five additional larger sending districts not in our original case study sample have also reversed their choice losses and at least some of them probably fall into the Change category. Four additional large senders fall into the No Effect category because of small relative effects on total enrollment. Therefore, a large majority of sending districts with 100 or more choice losses in 1994–95 appear to fit expected responses under the market thesis.

The three districts that experienced some adverse effects but did not improve their programs (No Change) also represent an expected response according to market dynamics. For a variety of reasons, including lack of information and poor management decisions, not all enterprises will succeed in a market environment. In a healthy market, however, only a small fraction of enterprises should fall into the No Change category at any one time, which appears to be the case in our study.

The No Change response also resembles an outcome predicted by critics of the market thesis: districts will be adversely affected by choice and will be powerless to prevent or reverse those effects. Their powerlessness arises either from (1) lack of resources, which will be exacerbated by choice losses, or (2) choice losses, driven by racial and social considerations, over which the school authorities have no control, rather than by school programs.

A decision about which of these two scenarios applies should depend on the evidence. The per pupil expenditure data in figure 5–4 shows that No Change senders are only slightly less funded than the Change senders in 1993, and indeed their expenditures grew more rapidly (because of foundation aid) than Change senders, and by 1995 the No Change senders have almost the same per pupil expenditures resources as Change districts. There is no indication here that the No Change group has less resources than the Change group to address program deficiencies. Additionally, staff interviews in the No Change districts indicate a state of indecisiveness more than an inability to change, and in fact the staff lacked consensus about whether choice losses had serious adverse effects on their programs.

Another finding here that is consistent with the critics' argument is that a large number of staff in the No Effect and No Change districts believe that choice transfers are racially and socially motivated (see chapter 6 for actual numbers). While these staff members may simply be repeating criticisms of choice heard elsewhere, their claims cannot be dismissed lightly given their leadership positions in high minority school districts. Indeed, our position is that the staff interviews should be taken at face value unless contradicted by equally or more valid data sources.

If these staff beliefs are wrong, then a lot of education is needed. In fact, this may reflect a system of beliefs that reinforces the status quo, justifies inaction, and becomes a self-fulfilling prophesy for losing districts: their programs are good, choice students leave because of race and not programs, and nothing needs to be done to bring these families back. Therefore, nothing is done and students continue to leave.

However, if the staff belief about racial motivation is substantiated, then the market competition thesis is seriously flawed, at least for some of the large sending districts in Massachusetts. We now turn to an evaluation of this claim.

CHAPTER SIX

VIEWS AND ATTITUDES ABOUT CHOICE

Anyone concerned about the future of school choice policy should be interested in the opinions and attitudes of those affected by the policy, because they are likely to influence that future. That is to say, they should be interested in the views of school administrators, parents, students, and citizens (i.e., taxpayers) about the interdistrict choice law—how it affects them, whether they support or oppose it, or how it might be changed to solve problems they see in its implementation.

As evaluators of the Massachusetts choice law, we are interested in all of these views, but the findings in chapters 4 and 5 demand a look at one type of information in particular. Because the families who use interdistrict choice are disproportionately white, and because administrators at some sending schools believe many of these transfers are racially motivated, we must examine the question of motivation before coming to a final conclusion about racial impacts and the applicability of the market competition thesis. Specifically, we are interested here in the reasons given by parents and students for changing from one school (or district) to another. We also must take into account the views of school district staff about family motivations. Not only are they close observers of the choice process, in many school districts they are personally acquainted with families in the choice program.

Given our interest in the applicability of the market thesis to school choice policies, the role of families is critical. The market thesis obviously will not apply if families fail to exercise their choice options, but it will also not apply if families make choices for reasons that are unrelated to school quality. If, instead, they make choices on racial or social grounds, then we should not expect market competition to improve the quality of public education.

Ideally, we would also have the opinions of parents and students who are *not* using the interdistrict choice program, and especially the reasons offered by minority parents. Possibilities include lack of awareness about the choice program, transportation problems, perceived discrimination, or simply satisfaction with their current school program. Unfortunately, such data are not available for this study, so we rely instead on a Massachusetts survey on school choice issues. This survey will allow us to compare attitudes toward and support of interdistrict choice for Massachusetts adults of all races and ethnicities.

The attitudes of families and citizens toward the choice law also raise the broader question of how educational quality should be defined and who should define it. Supporters of school choice give great weight to family opinions, since families are the consumers of education and their support is critical for any system to work. Educators may be more inclined to view educational quality as a technical matter requiring professional judgment, that of the educators themselves or at least education researchers. Sometimes we forget about the taxpayers who fund public education and who generally want these funds to be used effectively. Taxpayers may well be the most important party of all, because no matter what parents and educators think about choice or educational quality, taxpayers can make their judgment count at the ballot box.

Accordingly, in addition to investigating the reasons families change school districts, this chapter also examines the opinions and viewpoints of these groups regarding various aspects of the

Massachusetts choice policy. We will discuss parent and student satisfaction with their school of choice, general levels of support for or opposition to the choice law, and specific changes these groups might want to make in the law. Although we do not have extensive data on academic outcomes, our student survey also has some limited information about grade averages and college aspirations.

Parent Views

The parent survey had several purposes. First and foremost, we wanted to test differing assumptions about why parents change their children's school districts, and in particular to evaluate whether they were motivated mainly by academic, social, or racial reasons. If the market process is to benefit education, families should change schools for academic reasons or at least ancillary concerns, such as enforcement of rules and discipline.

Second, we wanted to discover whether parents were satisfied with their choice of school, to what extent they support the choice law, and their views about what modifications, if any, they want to see in the choice law. This information should help us to evaluate the overall success of the program, from the consumers' standpoint, and to recommend any changes that might help improve the effectiveness of the policy.

For some of the results discussed here, and in particular the reasons for transfers, we have combined the parent responses with those from the student survey. Other results from the student survey are discussed in a subsequent section.

Reasons for Transfer

The parent surveys included questions about the reasons their children transferred to the school they now attend. First, there was an open-ended question, that is, parents could offer reasons in their own words; a series of closed-end questions followed that listed 13 specific reasons. The reasons selected were based on pre-test interviews. During telephone interviews parents were asked to indicate whether each reason was a major, minor, or not a factor in their decision to choose their child's current school (or school district). A similar question was asked in the self-administered student questionnaire; the student survey was generally administered a week or two prior to the parent interviews.[1]

Figure 6–1 summarizes the results for the closed-end questions. It shows the percentage of parents and students indicating that a particular reason was a "major" factor in their decision to change schools. The responses clearly indicate the dominance of academic concerns for both groups. The number one reason, chosen by 83 percent of the parents and 63 percent of the students, was that the choice school had higher academic standards and/or was more challenging. The number two reason for both groups was diversity or quality of the curriculum, which was defined in the questionnaires as the existence or quality of specific courses.

After the first two most important reasons for transferring, parent and student reasons diverge somewhat. The next four most important reasons for parents are facilities, safety, smaller school, and teachers, in that order. The next four reasons for students are the same as for parents, but in a different order: safety, teachers, facilities, and smaller schools. Both groups put all the non-academic reasons such as convenience, athletics, activities, and friends at the bottom of the list of reasons.

Because of pre-test results, we did not list race or ethnicity as a reason in the closed-end questions; we thought it would be better to obtain this type of information from an open-end question. In a careful search of all open-ended responses of parents, we found only three parents, in three different schools, who mentioned race- or ethnic-related issues in relation to their change of schools.

---

[1] Students were asked the same set of reasons, except for the one on "change of environment."

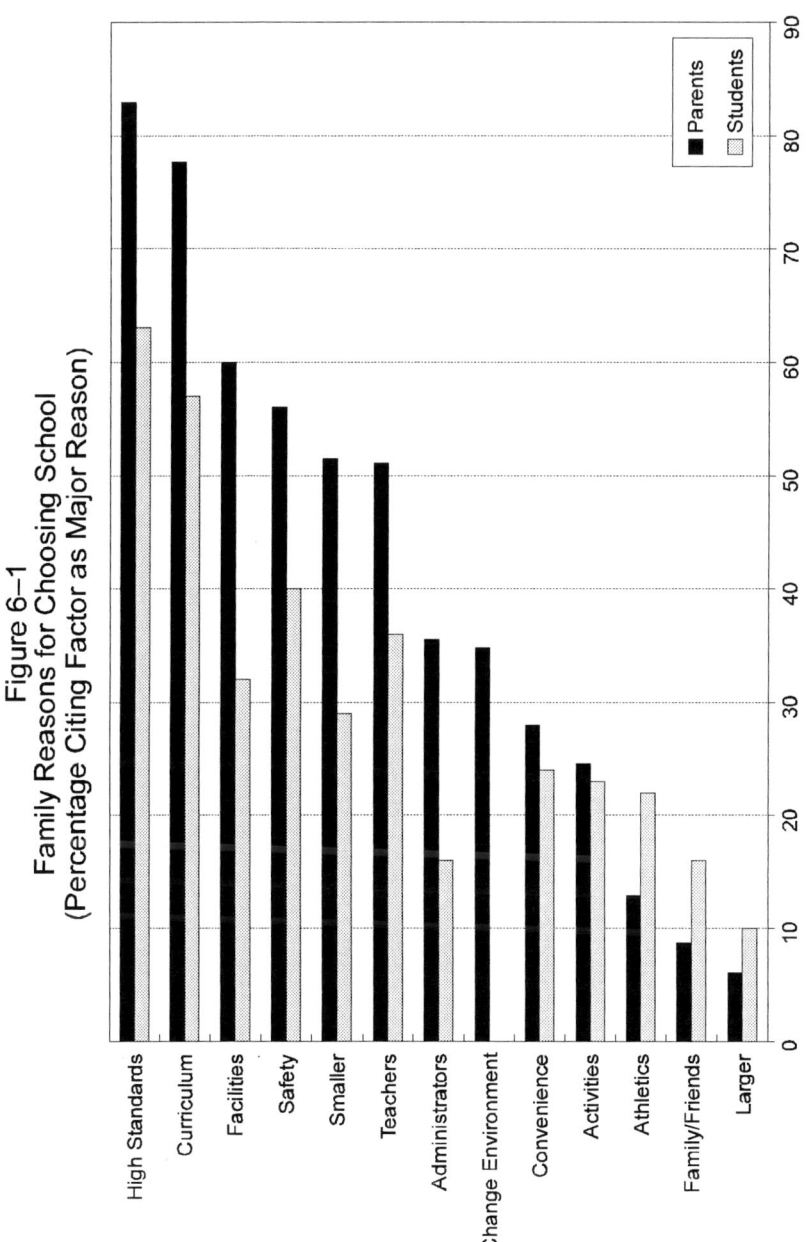

Figure 6–1
Family Reasons for Choosing School
(Percentage Citing Factor as Major Reason)

Some reasons, while seemingly not race-related, might represent conditions that are closely associated with concentrations of poor or minority students, such as "safety," which is the fourth most important reason for parents and third for students. In the open-end responses, terms like "crime," "violence," "gangs," or "drugs" were often used to illustrate safety concerns. Given national studies of urban schools that show a correlation between school violence and higher concentrations of poverty and minorities, it is possible that districts with higher violence and "safety" problems in our sample might also have higher minority enrollments. The question then becomes one of interpreting the true intentions of the parents who cite reasons of safety. Is it a racial concentration they are escaping or are they acting on a legitimate concern about safety in schools with higher rates of crime and violence?

We can examine the possible association between safety concerns and racial composition in table 6–1. It shows the number one and number two reasons given by parents for changing schools, listed separately for each receiving district, where each receiver is matched with its paired sender. Sending Districts 4 and 6 in the No Change group, all three of the No Effect districts, and sending District 10 have minority enrollments of over 15 percent, while sending District 5 and all of the Change districts are less than 5 percent minority. Of the top 12 reasons given by parents from the six higher minority senders, seven are higher standards or curriculum, two are size, and three are safety.

In other words, while safety is a major reason in some of the higher minority districts, academic reasons still provide the predominant motivation for choice according to parents from these districts. Moreover, the fact that safety is mentioned in half of the high minority districts does not in itself indicate racial motivation, provided that parents are truly concerned about violence, gangs, or drugs and not race. Although we have no way to test the truthfulness of these responses, we can look at the consistency of responses among subgroups of parents, students, and staff.[2]

Table 6–1
Parent Reasons for Choosing School, by District

Receiver	1st Reason	2nd Reason	Sender
			CHANGE
RECEIVER 1	High Standards	Curriculum	SENDER 1
RECEIVER 2	High Standards	Curriculum	SENDER 2
RECEIVER 3	Curriculum	High Standards	SENDER 3
			NO CHANGE
RECEIVER 4	Smaller (Tie)	Safety (Tie)	SENDER 1
RECEIVER 5	High Standards (Tie)	Smaller (Tie)	SENDER 2
RECEIVER 6	High Standards	Curriculum	SENDER 3
			NO EFFECT
RECEIVER 7	Curriculum	High Standards	SENDER 1
RECEIVER 8	Curriculum	High Standards	SENDER 2
RECEIVER 9	High Standards	Safety	SENDER 3
RECEIVER 10	Smaller	Safety	SENDER 10

For example, we can consider the reasons cited by nonwhite or lower SES parents. Table 6–2 shows the major reason for changing districts for five subgroups of parents: nonwhite, single parents, renters, lower income, and lower education. The results are ranked according to nonwhite responses. The ranking of reasons is virtually identical to the total sample for all five groups, with higher standards

---

[2] See figure 6–2 for staff reasons. In table 6–5, we show that safety is listed as the second reason in only one of the high minority districts.

as the number one reason and curriculum number two for all groups except renters, who reverse that order. We note that safety is the number four reason for nonwhite parents, as it is for the other low-SES subgroups.

In summary, all but one group discussed here cite academic quality as the major reason for transferring to another school, with remarkable agreement about two specific factors: high academic standards and curriculum.

Table 6–2
Parent Reasons for Choosing School,
by Parent Race and SES
(percent)

Major Reason	Nonwhite	One Parent	Renters	Income of <$35.000	Education HS or Less
High Academic Standards	86	84	75	81	73
Curriculum	68	73	80	73	73
Facilities	68	75	69	75	63
Safety	64	55	59	63	60
Teachers	64	50	46	42	40
Smaller	57	41	41	42	59
Administrators	39	36	34	40	41
Change	32	45	39	50	43
Activities	25	23	25	10	24
Convenience	25	27	24	21	33
Family/Friends	14	7	12	10	5
Larger	0	7	0	4	6
(N)	(28)	(48)	(59)	(48)	(63)

PARENT SATISFACTION AND SCHOOL OF ORIGIN

Several other results from the parent survey are useful in evaluating the success and viability of the choice program. First, parents are very happy about their school of choice and see their decision as relatively permanent. About 73 percent say they are very satisfied with their child's school (26 percent are somewhat satisfied), and 79 percent say that they definitely plan to keep their child in the present district until graduation (another 16 percent said they probably will).

Second, some critics of the Massachusetts interdistrict choice program have expressed concern that private and parochial school families can enroll in public schools other than those in their residence community, thereby requiring the sending district to subsidize students who were not even in their system. Although we did not ask that specific question, we did ask parents where they would send their children if the public school choice program were not available. About 47 percent said private or parochial schools (private 32 percent, parochial 15 percent), which suggests that a sizable number of these students would be attending private schools in the absence of the choice law.

There is another viewpoint that does not see such a result as inherently unfair or improper. Before choice, these parents were paying twice to educate their children, once as taxpayers in their home community and once for private school tuition. They are clearly not going to attend their home district (unless changes occur), and the community therefore receives a windfall by collecting taxes from these families but not paying the cost of educating their children. By the student's transferring to another public school district, paid for by the home district, the local funds collected (plus the state aid) are simply transferred to another public school district as well. Thus the choice family is now paying once for the child's education, and the home district loses its windfall.

SUPPORT OF LAW AND RECOMMENDED CHANGES

Finally, we consider the degree of parental support for the Massachusetts choice law and any recommended changes for improving the policy. Not surprisingly, parents are highly supportive of the choice law, with 88 percent saying they strongly support it and another 9 percent saying they support it somewhat. While supporting the law as-is, about 58 percent of the parents said that the choice law needed some improvements.

Table 6–3 tabulates parents' recommended changes to the law. The most frequent recommendation (42 percent) is to increase funds for transportation between districts. The state law currently provides transportation subsidy for low-income students, but the majority of transfers are not low-income and have to arrange and pay for their own transportation. The second most frequent recommendation (21 percent) is to make choice mandatory statewide, so that districts cannot opt out of receiving students (except for capacity reasons). Finally, while only about 15 parents mentioned more money for the choice program, more than half of these said that the sending district should not have to pay so much for choice students.

STUDENT VIEWS AND OUTCOMES

The student survey was conducted for essentially the same reasons as the parent survey. Most important, the student survey provides an independent replication of the reasons families give for changing schools or school districts and tests whether students offered reasons for changing schools that agreed with or differed from those given by their parents. In particular, we wanted to know whether students were motivated by academic or nonacademic factors, and especially whether there were any suggestions that racial prejudice might be involved.

Table 6-3
Parent Recommended Changes to the Choice Law

Recommendation	Percentage
Provide more transportation	42
Make choice mandatory statewide	21
More money to districts	9
Allow siblings to transfer	7
Improve choice school program	5
Increase information	5
Other	12
(N)	(177)

We also wanted to understand the student perspective on school choice, and to investigate some of the academic outcomes that can be ascertained through self-reports, such as grade averages and college aspirations.

The student perspectives of greatest interest were satisfaction with their current school, support of the choice law, and recommended changes to the law, if any. The student questionnaire was structured to be similar to the parent interview schedule, with both open- and closed-end questions about the reasons for choosing their current school. Students were asked to estimate their grade averages before and after changing schools, and also about their post-high school plans.

REASONS FOR TRANSFER

We have already discussed student responses to the closed-end questions on reasons for transfer (figure 6-1), and we noted that the leading reasons for transfers were higher academic standards and a stronger curriculum in the new school.

When students were asked the same question without a list from which to choose possible reasons, virtually the same responses were given. We coded these responses by applying the same categories that were used in the closed-end questions but were prepared to include additional categories, especially those mentioning race or ethnicity. In a thorough analysis of the closed-end responses, however, we found no mention of race or related concerns, nor did we find any other reasons that were not mentioned in the earlier list.

Table 6–4
Student Reasons for Choosing School, Open-End

Major Reason	Percent
High academic standards	64
Quality or diversity of courses	20
Safety	11
Teachers	10
Smaller school	9
Facilities and resources	8
Friends	6
Extracurricular activities	5
Athletics	5
Larger school	4
Convenience	3
(N)	(213)

The open-end responses are shown in table 6–4. The ranking of reasons is very similar to the ranking in figure 6–1, with 64 percent of students offering higher academic standards as the main reason they or their parents chose their present school. Only 5 percent of students chose athletics or extracurricular activities, and even fewer chose convenience or location as a reason for the switch.

Table 6–5
Student Reasons for Choosing School, By District

Receiver	1st Reason	2nd Reason	Major Sender
			CHANGE
RECEIVER 1	High Standards	Curriculum	SENDER 1
RECEIVER 2	Curriculum	High Standards	SENDER 2
RECEIVER 3	Curriculum	High Standards	SENDER 3
			NO CHANGE
RECEIVER 4	High Standards	Curriculum	SENDER 1
RECEIVER 5	High Standards	Smaller School	SENDER 2
RECEIVER 6	High Standards	Curriculum	SENDER 3
			NO EFFECT
RECEIVER 7	High Standards	Safety	SENDER 1
RECEIVER 8	High Standards	Curriculum	SENDER 2
RECEIVER 9	High Standards	Curriculum	SENDER 3
RECEIVER 10	High Standards	Smaller School	SENDER 10

Regardless of racial or family background, students in our survey offered a consistent response regarding their reasons for participation in the interdistrict choice program. Table 6–6 shows that nonwhite students—defined as African-American, Hispanic, Asian American, and Native American—were even stronger in their support of higher standards and better quality courses than were white students. About 89 and 72 percent of nonwhite students chose higher standards and a more challenging curriculum, respectively, as the primary reasons for the decision to leave their home district. While one-third of nonwhite students did choose athletics as a major reason, less than one-quarter chose location or the fact that their friends had also switched.

Table 6–6 indicates similar results for students who live in single-parent households and for students whose families do not own their home. Regardless of student background, higher standards and a more challenging curriculum are clearly the primary reasons for the decision to leave the home districts.

Table 6–6
Student Reasons for Choosing School, Closed-End
(percent)

Major Reason	Non-Whites	Single Parent Households	Renters
High academic standards	89	61	68
Quality or diversity of courses	72	50	61
Safety	44	36	37
Teachers	39	36	24
Smaller school	33	31	32
Athletics	33	22	17
Extracurricular activities	28	14	24
Facilities and resources	22	36	37
Convenience	22	22	24
Friends	22	22	13
Administrators	17	14	10
Larger school	11	14	13
(N)	(23)	(36)	(41)

STUDENT SATISFACTION

Students in our sample are highly satisfied with their decision to change schools. Nearly 90 percent of students surveyed reported being satisfied or very satisfied with their present school, while only 10 percent of students reported some degree of dissatisfaction. In addition, over 90 percent of students will likely or definitely stay in their choice district until they graduate.

SUPPORT FOR THE LAW AND RECOMMENDED CHANGES

Only one-third of students felt that there was anything the state could do to improve the school choice program. Of those who felt improvements could be made, 38 percent recommended that the state provide transportation for students wishing to choose another district (table 6–7). This is not surprising given that more than three-fifths of the sample students reported needing their own or a family member's car to get to school. As for other changes, nearly one-quarter of the respondents recommended that the state require all districts to participate in the school choice program.

Table 6–7
Student Recommended Changes to the Choice Law

Recommendation	Percentage
Provide more transportation	38
Make choice mandatory statewide	21
More money to districts	10
Improve choice programs	10
Increase information about choice	4
Other	8
(N)	(73)

Student Outcomes

We assessed two potential student outcomes in the student questionnaire. One is plans after graduation including college plans, and the other is change of grade average from their old to new school.

The students from our 10 receiving districts indicated a higher degree of aspiration than students in the state department of education's own study of Massachusetts students. According to the state office, 53 percent of students from the class of 1994 plan to attend a four-year college, while nearly 80 percent of our student sample indicate the same future plan. In fact, almost 90 percent of the students we interviewed intend to matriculate at either a two- or four-year college following graduation from high school (table 6–8).

We cannot make any inference that this was caused by the choice school, and in fact, we showed in chapter 4 that choice parents had higher average socioeconomic status than families statewide. This simply indicates that choice students have higher college aspirations than students statewide.

Table 6–8
Post-Graduation Plans
(percent)

Future Plan	Choice Sample	Statewide Sample[a]
Four-year college	79	53
Two-year college	9	19
Military	3	3
Full-time job	3	17
Other	6	7
(N)	(146)	(47,454)

[a] Massachusetts Department of Education, "Plans of High School Graduates, The Class of 1994," September 1995.

Given that the students in our sample indicated higher standards and a richer curriculum as the primary reasons for their choice to transfer, we would expect to see a change in their grade point averages. The results from our sample reflect just such a shift (table 6–9). While over half of the students reported receiving mostly As or a mix of As and Bs in the last year of their former school, only 41 percent indicated receiving those same high grades in their current choice school. Presumably, the higher standards that attracted students to their new district resulted in a 10 percent decline in the highest category of grades. This conclusion is buoyed by the 13 percent increase in the lower category of grades, mostly Bs or a mix of Bs and Cs, and lends further validity to the argument that higher or harder standards of grading do indeed exist at the receiving districts.

Table 6–9
Grade Average of Choice Students
(percent)

Grade	Previous School	Current School
Mostly As/Mixed As and Bs	51	41
Mostly Bs/Mixed Bs and Cs	28	41
Mostly Cs or lower	21	19
(N)	(184)	(184)

DISTRICT STAFF VIEWS

As revealed in chapter 5, a number of sending district staff stated that choice transfers from their districts are racially motivated. Given the very different picture of motivation painted by choice parents and students, it is important to consider systematically the views of all school district staff on this question. We will also discuss staff support of or opposition to the choice law and compare their recommendations for changes with those of choice families. Because of their different vantage points in the choice process, we will report results separately for net sending and receiving district staff members.

Figure 6-2 tabulates district staff responses to an open-ended question about their perceptions of the major reasons families either chose to attend or leave their district. There is broad disagreement between net receiving and net sending district staff about motivations for choice transfers. The dominant reason for transfers according to receiving district staff is higher academic standards, cited by 58 percent of staff, which is also the main reason offered by parents and students. Better curriculum is the second reason, mentioned by 17 percent of receiving district staff, again consistent with parent and student results. Small size and safety represent the third and fourth most important reasons for receiving district staff, which are the fifth and fourth reasons for parents, respectively. Thus staff and parents agree on four of the top five reasons for transfers, with complete agreement on the top two reasons.

For sending district staff the most frequent explanation for transfers out of the district is racial and ethnic motivation, cited by 31 percent. The second reason is facilities or funding (15 percent), and the third is safety concerns (12 percent). It should be noted that all mentions of race/ethnicity come from staff at the five districts with the highest minority enrollments (two No Change, three No Effect); no staff member at the other four sending districts mentioned racial motivation, and few mentioned anything but programmatic reasons.[3]

While we cannot eliminate the possibility that staff at the high minority sending districts are the only ones who are correctly perceiving family motivations while all others are either mistaken or masking their real reasons, we also must consider the possibility that

---

[3] District 10 staff were not interviewed, so we cannot classify this district with regard to staff perception of choice transfers.

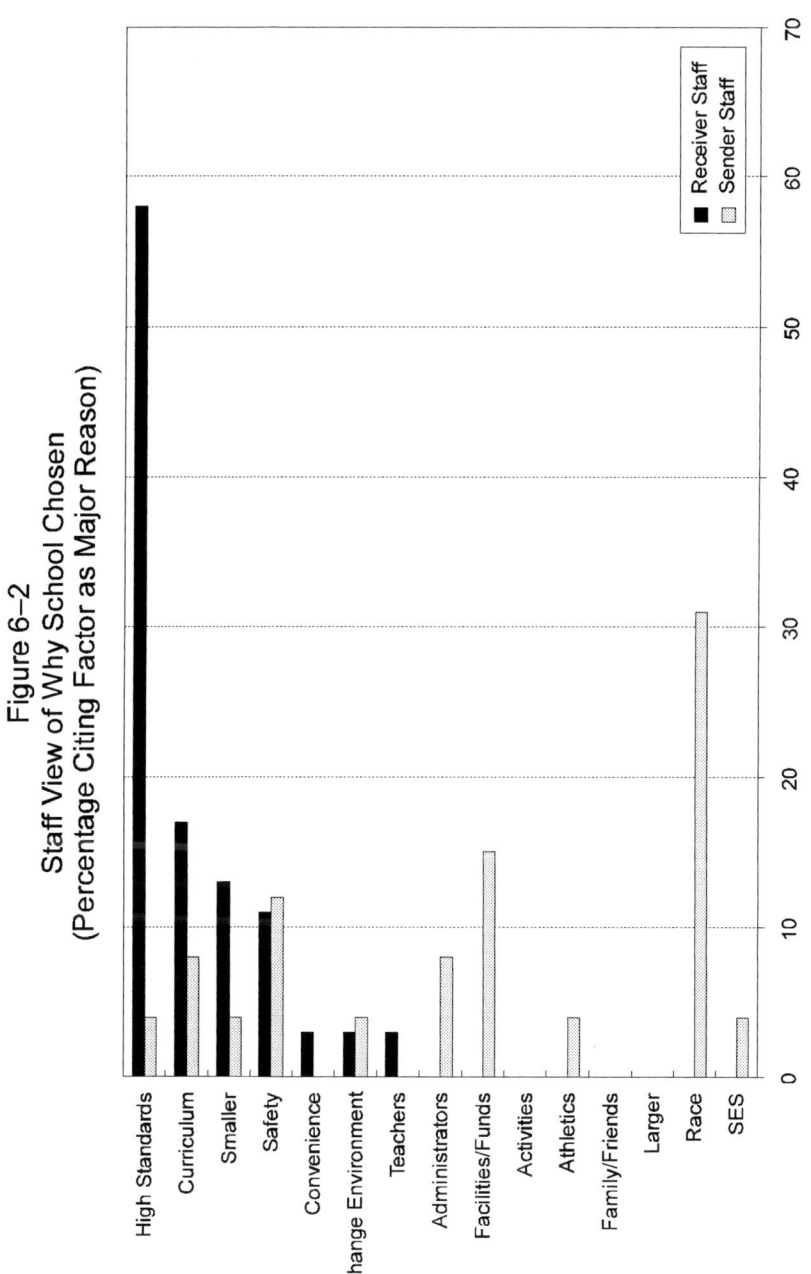

parents, students, receiving district staff, and staff from low minority sending districts have it right—that families are motivated by quality of programs. It may well be easier for some administrators and school committees to blame the loss of students on higher minority enrollments, over which they have little control, rather than on their academic standards and programs, for which they carry the burden of responsibility and accountability.

What about the opinions of staff in sending and receiving districts about the interdistrict choice law, and what are their proposals for changing the choice law, if any? We were surprised by the degree of variation in support for the choice law, and our initial assumption that as a group receiving district staff would be much more supportive than sending district staff proved to be incorrect.

Table 6–10 shows the percentage of receiving and sending district staff, by type of sender, who support the current choice law as-is, support the law but would like to see changes, or oppose the law. Remarkably, the Change staff show a higher degree of support for the choice law than receiving district staff, with 33 percent supporting unconditionally and only 17 percent opposing (versus 17 and 28 percent, respectively, for receiving districts).

The fact that the end result of choice turned adversity into advantage for the Change senders may be responsible for their level of support. It is quite possible that the sending district staff who ultimately benefited from choice recognize, more than staff from any other group of districts, that they would not have been able to improve their academic program had they not experienced the initial adversity brought on by choice losses.

Surprisingly, the No Effect staff also shows a high degree of support for the choice law, although most of the supporters would like to see changes. It might be that the lack of perceived impacts of choice losses (except on diversity) minimizes the degree of outright opposition to the choice law. As we shall see, many of these staff do suggest that the law be changed to prevent adverse race and ethnic impacts, which reveals the greatest concern about diversity of all the district groupings.

Table 6–10
School Staff Views of the Choice Law
(percent)

Type of District	Support As-Is	Support, Would Like Some Changes[a]	Oppose[b]	(N)
SENDERS				
Change	33	50	17	(12)
No Change	0	14	86	(7)
No Effect	9	45	45	(11)
All senders	17	41	42	(29)
RECEIVERS	17	56	28	(36)

[a] Support does not depend on making the change.
[b] Oppose outright or oppose but might consider support if changes made.

The group with the greatest opposition to the choice law is the No Change group. This outcome might be explained by the fact that, like the Change group, many staff in these districts see significant adverse effects, but unlike the Change group they see few benefits from the law because they have seen few significant improvements following the negative impact. In short, the No Change group has experienced pain but no gain.

Finally, it is interesting that the substantial benefits of choice for receiving districts do not translate into particularly strong levels of support for the choice law. A number of receiver staff expressed sentiments similar to critics of choice, particularly that they had reservations about the current choice law because it was taking money away from districts that were already disadvantaged.

Opposition to choice was particularly strong in one receiving district that had voted to terminate the choice program shortly before our site visit. This district accounts for 4 of the 10 responses in opposition to the choice law, and if this district is eliminated from table 6–10, the percentage of opposition among receivers would be similar to the percentage for the Change group. The majority of these staff members said the reason for termination was the perceived adverse impacts of choice on the primary sending district, coupled with their view that they did not need the choice money to sustain a high-quality program. This is the only receiving district to report few benefits from choice.

Table 6–11 summarizes the various recommendations from district staff for changing the choice law. For the most part the major recommendations differ from those of parents and students. The most frequent proposal from both sending and receiving district staff is to reduce the financial impact on senders, usually by having the state pay more or all of the tuition costs. Many receiving district administrators were clearly uncomfortable with tuition payments coming out of sending district budgets, particularly those with higher proportions of disadvantaged students, even though they liked the financial benefits of choice. More than one said something like, "It's like kicking someone when their down," or "It's like penalizing the victim." This does not mean they wanted to receive less in tuition payments; they simply wanted to shift more of the burden back to the state.

Money also figures in the second most frequent proposal by receiving district staff, which was to increase the tuition payments to receivers. Most respondents making this recommendation complained about the cap of 75 percent on tuition (up to $5,000) as being insufficient compensation given their per pupil costs. Most of these respondents also believed that this increase should come from the state. Many respondents in both groups had no problem with increasing the taxpayer burden, in part because they believe that education is the state's responsibility in the first place. It should be noted, however, that many other receiving district staff said that the tuition they received was more than enough to pay for the marginal cost of educating choice students in their current program, leaving a bonus for additional special programs.

Table 6–11
Staff Proposals for the Choice Law
(percent)

Proposal	Receiving Districts	Sending Districts
Less money paid by senders	38	46
More money paid to receivers	24	0
More transportation subsidies	21	14
Mandatory for all districts	0	7
Abolish law	3	11
Add controls for students transferring[a]	6	21
No specific changes	12	14
Other	18	14
(N)	(34)	(28)

[a] Racial controls for senders.

The second most frequent recommendation made by sending district staff is to place controls on the type of student who can transfer. For most of the staff who made this suggestion, the main goal was to prevent adverse racial impacts, such as worsened racial balance or increased racial concentrations in the sending district. Of the six respondents who made this suggestion, five were from the No Effect districts.

The third most common recommendation for both groups is increased transportation subsidies. While state policy does include a subsidy for low-income choice students, many districts complain that they do not see that money for a long time. Other districts believe that all students should receive some type of support.

Finally, there were a number of "other" suggestions made by various respondents, but one of the "other" reasons deserves mention because five receiving district staff raised it: screening choice applicants before admitting them or terminating them after admission. The main concern here was to be able to refuse choice students who might have difficulty with academic levels or discipline codes, or to terminate serious behavior problems after students enroll.

CITIZEN VIEWS ON SCHOOL CHOICE

Most school policies, and certainly those that require public funding, will ultimately be judged by voting citizens at large, either by direct votes on referenda or by their election of representatives at state and local levels. For this reason, comprehensive evaluations of a particular choice policy requires consideration of the views of the average citizen.

The views of residents play an additional role in this study. Since we do not have survey information from parents who did not transfer under the interdistrict choice program, we can use the Massachusetts survey to look for clues that might explain why minority students are underrepresented in the interdistrict choice population either in comparison to statewide or sending district enrollment.[4]

---

[4] *Massachusetts Attitudes Concerning School Choice,* Boston: Pioneer Institute for Public Policy Research, August 1996.

The Massachusetts survey was designed to assess opinion on a variety of school choice issues, including opinions about public and private education, belief in various principles and assumptions made by both proponents and opponents of choice, and support for specific types of choice plans. In addition, the survey over-sampled adults in the 10 largest cities in Massachusetts and minorities in the city of Boston.

Before discussing specific views on choice, general citizen views on education in Massachusetts provide helpful background. The average citizen does not give very high grades to the public schools in their own community, with about half saying A or B but 40 percent saying C or worse. When asked about public schools throughout the state, only 22 percent say A or B, 42 percent C, and 15 percent D or F.

This rather uncharitable view of the public schools is reinforced by responses to the next question, which is whether they would send a child to public or private/parochial schools if cost were no object. Only 26 percent said public, while 71 percent said private or parochial. Private and parochial were also the dominant responses of urban parents (73 percent) and minority parents (65 percent).

With this backdrop of general public opinion, it is not surprising that proposals to increase school choice are generally supported. Indeed, 61 percent of adults statewide agreed that increased school choice should improve the public schools in Massachusetts, and only 35 percent disagreed. About 60 percent of white adults agreed with this, but an even higher percent of minority adults, 65 percent, said that increased choice would improve school quality.[5]

---

[5] These and other racial/ethnic comparisons in the tables are based on 585 white, 128 black, and 87 other minority adults.

Citizen views on basic principles and assumptions behind the choice process should affect their views about how to expand school choice. It may also reveal differences between white and minority adults about some of the potential adverse effects of choice.

Table 6–12 shows the percentage of citizens who agree with certain assumptions about the educational, social, and economic effects of school choice broken down by race. Generally, large majorities of white citizens agree with the stated benefits of increased school choice and disagree with the stated harms, although 45 percent expect that economic and racial segregation will increase. They agree most strongly with the statement that choice will improve education through accountability, efficiency, and cost-effectiveness. Black residents agree even more strongly that choice will improve education for poor and minority students and will create more cost-effective schools, but a majority (53 percent) also believe that choice will increase economic and racial segregation. A majority of other minority respondents agree with the stated benefits of choice but show higher levels of concern about negative effects. Generally, it appears that Massachusetts residents of all races agree more with the pro-choice than anti-choice arguments.

The most important opinions for our purposes are residents' support for specific school choice plans, including interdistrict choice, and how these views compare for white, black, and other minority residents. The plans tested in the survey are interdistrict public school choice, charter schools, and voucher payments for all public and private schools.

As shown in table 6–13, a majority of all racial groups support all three types of choice programs, but the ranking of support differs somewhat by group. About two-thirds of white adults support both charter schools and vouchers, but their support drops off somewhat for interdistrict choice (59 percent). African-American adults endorse both interdistrict choice and charter schools more strongly than whites (about three-fourths supporting), but support drops off for vouchers (63 percent). A majority of other minority adults support all three choice options but at somewhat lower levels than white or black adults (except they are about equal to whites in support for interdistrict choice).

Table 6–12
Citizen Views about the Impact of School Choice

INCREASED CHOICE WILL	WHITE	BLACK	OTHER
Improve education for poor and minorities	69	81	71
Divide people	38	38	47
Cause more bad choices	31	40	45
Increase economic and racial segregation	45	53	53
Improve the quality of education through accountability	77	79	70
Force schools to be more cost-effective and efficient	75	83	66

(Percent Agreeing with Statement)

There is strong evidence in the citizen survey that African-American adults are more supportive of interdistrict choice than adults statewide, and that other minorities are as supportive as white adults. We would expect, therefore, that minority families would have as much interest in using interdistrict choice as white families, provided they are aware of the program and there are no obstacles that hamper their participation. Indeed, this is precisely what is happening in both the METCO and charter school programs.

Table 6–13
Citizen Support for Three Choice Plans
(percent)[a]

Plan	White	Black	Other
Interdistrict choice	59	75	57
Charter schools	65	76	56
State vouchers for all schools	66	69	59

[a] These questions were asked both before and after the agree-disagree questions about specific effects of choice. This table uses the responses to the second series.

CONCLUSIONS

The most important finding from this analysis concerns the reasons families change school districts. Our data generally contradict critics of choice who claim that parents will leave higher minority or poverty districts for reasons related to race or class, thereby undermining the applicability of market concepts to public schools.

The vast majority of choice parents and students of all backgrounds, staff at receiving districts, and even staff at lower minority sending districts cite academic and programmatic features as the main reasons for choosing a particular school district. The most important of these programmatic features is simply academic standards, which families believe to be higher in their schools of choice than in their home districts.

The most intriguing aspect of this particular criticism of sending districts is that, of all of the school policies and programs that figure in school quality, maintaining high academic standards is the least expensive. It can be accomplished without adding teachers, without new facilities, without buying new equipment, and without designing new courses. It is accomplished primarily by policy and by teaching practices, requiring that teachers hold to a relatively high standard of content and performance regardless of the academic ability of their students, without compensating for lower ability students either by adjusting grading practices or watering down course content. In other words, it is accomplished by avoiding teaching to the lowest common denominator.

We must acknowledge, of course, that most administrative staff in higher minority sending districts believe that the principal motivation for transfers out is race-related, either to avoid desegregation policies or to avoid contact with high minority concentrations. We also note that safety was mentioned as a major reason by parents in some but not all of the higher minority districts, although we cannot assume this represents simply racial prejudice masked by false concerns about gangs and violence, given the realities faced by many high minority urban school districts.

While we cannot prove that the majority of parents, students, and other district staff are being honest and more accurate about motivations, we also have to consider the possibility that sending staff in high minority districts are misperceiving the true motivations of most parents. We have to weigh the possibility that the belief in racial motivation allows them to continue with business as usual, avoiding assessment of what is happening in classrooms that could explain these losses and validate the reasons given by parents and students.

Finally, while the weight of evidence supports a nonracial interpretation for choice moves, we are nonetheless concerned that minority families are underrepresented in the interdistrict choice population. The fact that the adult survey shows strong support of and interest in expanded choice options on the part of both urban and minority parents, coupled with the documented high rates of participation of minority students in METCO and charter schools, suggests to us that it is not a lack of interest in interdistrict choice but rather barriers of some type. Although we have no definitive data on exactly what these barriers might be, it is possible that minority families are either unaware of interdistrict choice options in their area or are hampered by lack of transportation services.

With respect to transportation issues, we note that transportation assistance was the number one recommendation of both parents and students for improving the choice program. If transportation is an issue for the current choice population, which is generally more affluent than the nonchoice sender population, then it must be an even bigger issue for low-income families. While the state does offer transportation assistance for low-income families, it may be that many eligible minority families are not aware of it.

CHAPTER SEVEN

CONCLUSIONS AND POLICY RECOMMENDATIONS

Three policy questions about choice—racial impacts, the market competition thesis, and choice family motivations—have been studied here as separate issues, but they are clearly interrelated. The answers to the first two depend at least partially on the third, because both involve assumptions about the behavior of families. In fact, the most important philosophical divide between proponents and critics of school choice has to do with different viewpoints about human motivation and behavior as manifested in the realm of schooling.

The proponents of school choice who apply market concepts to education see families and schools in the public sector as no different than consumers and businesses in the private sector. As consumers of education, families will act rationally in their choice of schools to maximize benefits for their children and minimize costs, and the ultimate impact of these choices will improve school quality because schools must offer a good product (program) in order to retain market share (enrollment) and stay in business.

For this argument to work, two conditions must be met. First, families must see benefits and costs in academic rather than social terms. That is, parents must choose another school system because it has a better academic program, not because it has a lower concentration of poor and minority families. Under this scenario, poor and minority families should behave in the same way as affluent and white families, and they should also seek the best school programs provided there are no artificial barriers. Second, public school systems must be free to improve their programs in response to enrollment losses by raising funds (if necessary) and by being free to make the necessary programmatic decisions to meet family demands.

While critics of school choice do not necessarily renounce market concepts per se, they reject their applicability to public education. Again, central to their conclusions are different assumptions about the motivation of families and the tractability of public school systems. First, while families may try to maximize benefits for their children and minimize costs, critics say they will evaluate schools along social and racial rather than academic lines. If given unconstrained choice, middle-class and white families will leave high minority urban districts for less minority and more affluent suburban communities, not so much to improve their educational opportunities but to find a more compatible social milieu. The end result is increasing social and racial isolation of school systems that are already socially and racially imbalanced.

Second, to the extent that families leave because of weak programs, school systems that lose students are unable to improve their programs because they are public entities with fixed budgets and are trapped by regulations. In fact, choice losses further reduce their limited resources, making it even more difficult to improve their programs. Thus the only result of unconstrained choice is the loss of middle-class families, leaving behind an increasingly disadvantaged student population.

The findings presented in chapters 4 to 6 shed considerable light on these issues, at least as they apply to interdistrict public school choice in Massachusetts. While this assessment does not answer every question definitively, a fairly clear picture has emerged as to which of these two points of view is most consistent with the evidence at hand.

Aside from the validation of various theories about the impact of school choice, the findings here also have some definite policy implications, some of which need to be addressed soon by Massachusetts policy makers. Our recommendations follow the summary of major findings.

MAJOR FINDINGS

The findings of this study are generally consistent with the arguments and assumptions made by proponents of choice, with one important exception. The most important finding is that the Massachusetts choice law demonstrates the applicability of the market competition thesis to public schools. The exception concerns the social and racial representativeness of the interdistrict choice population.

Turning first to the market competition thesis, we found that a majority of large net sending school districts in our case studies responded to choice losses or gains in ways expected in a competitive market situation. The sending districts with the largest relative enrollment and financial losses due to choice responded by making programmatic changes in an attempt to stop or recover these losses. Not only did these districts respond according to market theory, these changes were effective in recovering some or all of the lost market share. The experience of turning serious adversity—if not disaster— into substantial advantage also generated considerable support for the choice law on the part of the leadership in these districts. Enrollment data for other large net sending districts not in our case studies are also consistent with the market thesis, showing that other districts with the largest relative losses have been able to reverse these losses.

Other large net sending districts fit an appropriate market response because the leadership did not perceive serious adverse effects from choice losses, and therefore the school district felt no need to improve its programs. State data confirm the very small effects of choice and tuition losses for these districts as a percentage of total enrollment or total expenditures, mainly because of large enrollments.

In only one respect do the staff in these sending districts, all of which have higher minority enrollments, conform to the critics' model: they believe that choice families left their districts because of racial motivations, including the escape from integration plans. Since the preponderance of information from parent, student, and receiver staff fails to confirm this belief, we belief that this viewpoint is incorrect. Indeed, this belief may serve to justify the status quo and prevent school leadership from evaluating the criticism of parents who leave their districts.

Several school districts experienced some adverse effects but made no significant attempt to assess and modify their programs. On the one hand, these cases fit an expected pattern under the critics' thesis, which is adverse effects coupled with inability to change. On the other hand, the staff interviews suggest the problem is indecision and lack of consensus about effects more than some structural inability to change. Indeed, market theory anticipates failure for some proportion of enterprises, not because of management's inability to change, but rather its lack of self-assessment and a decisive plan of action to resolve problems. Moreover, we also found that these districts had higher rates of increase in per pupil expenditures than other senders, undoubtedly due to the foundation aid. Therefore, these districts probably had less financial incentive than other senders to improve their programs.

Our evaluation also concludes that, for the most part, families who change school districts are behaving consistent with market principles. Our surveys of parents and students and our interviews with school staff suggest strongly that the motivation for changing districts is predominantly academic, with the most important reason being higher academic standards and better curriculum. This reason predominated not only among parents but also students, receiving district staff, staff in low minority sending districts, and subgroups of minority parents and students. Aside from being consistent with the market thesis, this finding also eliminates a major argument of choice critics, which is that choice families who leave high minority school districts are motivated primarily by social or racial concerns rather than by academics.

This brings us to our important exception, a finding that is consistent with the argument of choice critics. The interdistrict choice population generally tends to be less minority, higher SES, and higher achieving than the nonchoice population attending school in the sending districts, and students generally transfer from poorer, high minority districts with lower academic profiles to more affluent, low minority districts with higher academic profiles. We stress that this statement applies to the *average* choice student, and that there are some sending-receiving relationships in which either the schools are very similar or the choice students are less advantaged than those in the sending district as a whole.

The study does not find, however, that choice has serious adverse effects on racial balance or on the financial status of higher minority sending districts. While the interdistrict choice enrollment is not representative of sending district enrollment, the number of choice students is generally small in comparison to the total enrollments of high minority sending districts. Therefore, the loss of choice students has no appreciable impact on either the racial composition of higher minority sending districts or their overall financial status at this time.

The study also finds that the representation problem is confined to the interdistrict choice program. If we consider all choice students who leave their resident school district, including METCO and charter school students, we find that the total choice population is representative of the statewide Hispanic population and actually overrepresents the statewide African-American population.

The strong interest in school choice demonstrated by minority student participation in METCO and charter schools and the strong expression of support on the part of minority parents in the citizen survey convince us that the minority representation issue is an important problem but not fatal to the interdistrict choice program. Since minority families are just as interested as white families in using choice to increase their educational opportunities, as indicated by the resident survey and their participation in other school choice programs, the most likely explanation for underrepresentation in the interdistrict choice program is barriers of some type.

One possible barrier is restricted access, since less than one-third of Massachusetts districts are receivers at the present time. We note that making interdistrict choice mandatory for all districts was the second most frequent recommendation of choice families. A second possible barrier is insufficient transportation assistance, which is the top problem cited by both parents and students. A third possibility is simply lack of awareness of choice options—including transportation assistance—by minority and low-income parents. Advertising activities of receiving districts are relatively minimal at the present time, in most cases limited to local newspaper announcements. These potential barriers are addressed in our policy recommendations.

POLICY RECOMMENDATIONS

There is ample evidence in this study for recommending that the Massachusetts interdistrict choice program be continued, albeit with some modifications. The evidence in its favor includes the facts that many thousands of families are using it, they are very happy with it, and it has led to significant program improvements in some of the most impacted sending districts. It is also supported by a majority of school staff in our case study districts.

Moreover, there is no reason to impose racial restrictions on choice transfers. While the interdistrict choice population underrepresents minority families at this time, a condition that should be addressed, choice is having no significant adverse impact on racial balance, and indeed in some cases choice has actually improved it. Moreover, the vast majority of choice families are changing districts for academic and not race-related reasons, which not only mitigates the potential issue of intent, but provides further validation that market forces will continue to improve the quality of education. In order to obtain maximum benefits from these dynamics, it is essential that there be as few restrictions on choice as possible.

Based on our findings, we recommend five modifications to the choice law or its implementation. Four are aimed at improving the representation of minority and low-income families and the fifth is aimed at improving the competitive environment so that the benefits of choice will be fully realized.

1. AWARENESS ASSESSMENT

The state should conduct a survey to assess the interest in and awareness of interdistrict choice options among public school parents, especially minority and low-income families. The survey should also test awareness and adequacy of current transportation subsidies for low-income families.

2. TRANSPORTATION

Given the frequency of transportation complaints from choice families and school staff, the state should evaluate the adequacy of the present transportation assistance, particularly with regard to its adequacy for low-income families. The evaluation should include funding levels, timeliness and means of reimbursement, and any other regulations that may impede the efficient delivery of transportation assistance.

3. ADVERTISING

In order to improve awareness of choice options, all school districts should be required to inform any adjacent (or nearby) districts of the number of seats available for choice transfers, as well as advertise in local newspapers. All districts should be required to inform their own resident students of which adjacent (or nearby) school districts have seats available for choice transfers, as well as the availability of transportation.

4. ACCESS

To improve accessibility of interdistrict choice for low-income and minority parents, and to maximize the benefits of choice for all families and school systems in the state, all school districts should be required to accept choice students if there is space available. School boards would retain control over the determination of physical capacity, although capacity should not be manipulated to keep out students from other districts. We note that mandatory district participation in no way impairs local control over curriculum, academic standards, and staffing decisions.

5. TUITION PAYMENTS

All reimbursement for tuition losses should be phased out within a year or two after making choice mandatory for all districts. Since foundation aid is already increasing the funding of low-wealth school districts to put them on a par with all districts, there is less need to offer special reimbursements for below-foundation districts as foundation goals are realized over the next several years. For the market to work properly, there need to be clear financial rewards and penalties for gaining or losing market share, and the reimbursement system tends to work against market forces.

There is widespread misperception about the financial harms and benefits of the choice program. When a student enrolls in a school, almost everyone agrees that tuition should be set at per pupil expenditures, which is the assumed cost of educating that student. When a student leaves a school, no one acknowledges there is a saving from *not* having to educate that student, which should be similar to the assumed cost. Thus tuition payments not only represent incurred costs for receiving districts, they should also represent cost savings for sending districts. Accordingly, a study of marginal, variable, and fixed costs would be in order for Massachusetts schools. Based on such as study, one might then develop a general formula for tuition payments that is based on the actual marginal costs (or savings) for educating additional (or fewer) students, plus some reward for attracting students.

The current interdistrict choice law is a beneficial policy, which could be made better by improving racial and economic representation and by fine-tuning the funding formulas. If the recommendations about access, awareness, and transportation are adopted, it is likely that the interdistrict choice program will continue to grow beyond its current levels and possibly approach the higher participation levels of Iowa, Minnesota, and Washington, which are on the order of 2 to 3 percent of total enrollment. Even with these changes, the Massachusetts interdistrict choice population is not likely to reach the current 2 percent cap in the near future.

APPENDIX A

CHOICE TRENDS FOR STUDY DISTRICTS

152 COMPETITION IN EDUCATION

CHOICE TRENDS FOR STUDY DISTRICTS

NAME	TRANSFERS OUT				TRANSFERS IN			
	1993	1994	1995	1996	1993	1994	1995	1996
RECEIVER 1	0	0	0	0	171	205	228	217
RECEIVER 2	28	20	0	25	129	176	183	153
RECEIVER 3	4	13	13	11	269	314	313	294
RECEIVER 4	15	25	39	34	97	132	133	124
RECEIVER 5	8	11	8	5	174	152	138	133
RECEIVER 6	1	2	1	1	0	0	140	111
RECEIVER 7	29	39	46	45	89	144	136	146
RECEIVER 8	10	12	11	9	185	247	284	311
RECEIVER 9	0	2	2	2	3	69	133	106
RECEIVR 10	20	29	52	59	53	235	198	175
SENDER 1	121	114	98	80	21	33	36	29
SENDER 2	115	142	135	118	12	16	33	42
SENDER 3	82	135	105	88	39	44	79	100
SENDER 4	141	139	145	129	0	0	0	0
SENDER 5	38	133	187	220	37	75	66	74
SENDER 6	81	137	171	201	0	0	65	79
SENDER 7	78	154	154	159	0	3	26	45
SENDER 8	59	74	154	147	0	0	0	0
SENDER 9	158	284	258	292	0	0	0	0
SENDER 10	141	166	188	190	0	0	0	0
TOTAL	988	1465	1579	1625	1279	1845	2191	2139

NET TRANSFER GAINS/LOSSES (NUMBER)					NET TUITION GAINS/LOSSES ($000)			
	1993	1994	1995	1996	1993	1994	1995	1996
RECEIVER 1	171	205	228	217	688	871	896	954
RECEIVER 2	101	156	183	128	450	623	729	619
RECEIVER 3	265	301	300	283	842	873	1072	1051
RECEIVER 4	82	107	94	90	219	204	204	225
RECEIVER 5	166	141	130	128	788	651	643	663
RECEIVER 6	0	0	139	110	-2	-3	582	530
RECEIVER 7	60	105	90	101	228	296	287	312
RECEIVER 8	175	235	273	302	797	1040	1162	1269
RECEIVER 9	3	67	131	104	11	303	473	456
RECEIVR 10	33	206	146	116	188	566	478	436
SENDER 1	-100	-81	-62	-51	-343	-247	-219	-196
SENDER 2	-103	-126	-102	-76	-417	-542	-423	-378
SENDER 3	-43	-91	-26	12	-156	-255	-156	-110
	-82	-99	-63	-38				
SENDER 4	-141	-139	-145	-129	-655	-567	-655	-568
SENDER 5	-1	-58	-121	-146	-42	-179	-359	-506
SENDER 6	-81	-137	-106	-122	203	-434	-385	-419
	-74	-111	-124	-132				
SENDER 7	-78	-151	-128	-114	-255	-475	-454	-422
SENDER 8	-59	-74	-154	-147	-244	-286	-598	-652
SENDER 9	-158	-284	-258	-292	-480	-976	-955	-1118
	-98	-170	-180	-184				
SENDER 10	-141	-166	-188	-190	-566	-699	-739	-831

TUITION PAID ($000)				TUITION RECEIVED ($000)			
1993	1994	1995	1996	1993	1994	1995	1996
0	0	0	0	688	871	896	954
113	94	0	101	563	717	729	720
16	25	33	34	858	898	1105	1085
54	76	121	102	272	280	326	327
33	29	25	12	821	680	668	675
2	3	4	4	0	0	586	534
69	86	123	126	298	381	410	438
	52	61	67	797	1092	1223	1336
0	8	7	8	11	311	480	464
	89	153	193	188	656	631	629
397	317	324	296	54	71	105	100
462	581	534	531	45	39	111	153
263	363	373	362	107	108	217	252
655	567	655	568	0	0	0	0
146	366	546	722	104	187	188	216
283	434	551	741	0	0	166	292
255	477	498	536	0	2	44	114
244	286	598	652	0	0	0	0
480	976	955	1118	0	0	0	0
566	699	739	831	0	0	0	0

TOTAL DISTRICT ENROLLMENT				PER PUPIL EXPENDITURE ($)			
1993	1994	1995	1996	1993	1994	1995	1996
771	795	801	804	5766	5481	5699	5615
1025	1047	1023	1059	6465	5842	6065	6006
2891	2902	2951	3037	4189	4461	4757	5062
1713	1739	1747	1858	4120	4019	4316	4265
829	857	850	827	5218	5463	7085	7075
2534	2763	2813	2678	5379	5567	5445	5987
1664	1812	1929	1975	3584	3756	4136	4402
1843	1906	1921	1987	6744	6443	6374	6614
3156	3291	3358	3264	6503	6334	6300	5613
2828	2898	2973	3158	5818	4764	4625	4653
				5379	5213	5480	5529
1694	1865	1875	2108	4598	4803	4843	4480
1189	1256	1285	1358	5712	5878	5945	6018
1898	1958	2046	2204	3632	4199	4273	4450
				4647	4960	5020	5116
3613	3711	3712	3750	4522	5233	5595	5608
4837	4864	4916	5174	4238	4572	5034	5147
5337	5544	5900	6043	4141	4116	4160	4321
				4300	4640	4930	5025
7461	7726	7870	8029	3971	4214	4497	4860
12132	12521	13039	13703	4414	4521	4845	5283
22505	22638	25867	24213	4911	5020	5209	5879
				4432	4585	4850	5341
13742	14016	14391	14791	4096	4672	4983	5449

154 COMPETITION IN EDUCATION

NET TRANSFERS AS % OF TOTAL ENROLLMENT					NET TUITION AS % OF EXPENDITURES				
	1993	1994	1995	1996	1993	1994	1995	1996*	*1995 Data
RECEIVER 1	28.5	34.7	39.8	37.0	18.3	25.0	21.1	26.8	
RECEIVER 2	10.9	17.5	21.8	13.7	7.3	11.3	13.3	10.8	
RECEIVER 3	10.1	11.6	11.3	10.3	7.5	7.2	8.3	7.3	
RECEIVER 4	5.0	6.6	5.7	5.1	3.2	3.0	2.8	2.9	
RECEIVER 5	25.0	19.7	18.1	18.3	22.3	16.2	11.9	12.8	
RECEIVER 6	0.0	0.0	5.2	1.3	0.0	0.0	4.0	3.4	
RECEIVER 7	3.7	6.2	4.9	5.4	4.0	4.5	3.7	3.7	
RECEIVER 8	10.5	14.1	16.6	17.9	6.9	9.3	10.5	10.7	
RECEIVER 9	0.1	2.1	4.1	3.3	0.1	1.5	2.3	2.6	
RECEIVR 10	1.2	7.7	5.2	3.8	1.2	1.3	3.6	3.1	
	9.5	12.0	13.3	11.9	7.1	8.2	8.5	8.4	
SENDER 1	5.6	4.2	3.2	2.4	4.2	2.7	2.1	1.9	
SENDER 2	-8.0	-9.1	-7.4	-5.3	-5.8	-6.8	-5.2	-4.4	
SENDER 3	-2.2	-4.4	-1.3	0.5	-2.2	-3.0	-1.8	-1.1	
	-5.3	-5.9	-3.9	-2.4	-4.1	-4.2	-3.1	-2.5	
SENDER 4	-3.8	-3.6	-3.8	-3.3	-3.9	-2.8	-3.1	-2.6	
SENDER 5	0.0	-1.2	-2.4	-2.7	-0.2	-0.8	-1.1	-1.9	
SENDER 6	-1.5	-2.4	-1.8	-2.0	-1.3	-1.9	-1.5	-1.7	
	-1.8	-2.4	-2.6	-2.7	-1.8	-1.8	-2.0	-2.1	
SENDER 7	-1.0	-1.9	-1.6	-1.4	-0.5	-1.4	-1.3	-1.1	
SENDER 8	-0.5	-0.6	-1.2	-1.1	-0.5	-0.5	-0.9	-0.9	
SENDER 9	-0.7	-1.2	-1.0	-1.1	-0.4	-0.9	-0.7	-0.8	
	-0.7	-1.2	-1.3	-1.2	-0.6	-0.9	-1.0	-0.9	
SENDER 10	-1.0	-1.2	-1.3	-1.3	-1.0	-1.1	-1.0	-1.0	

SUMMARY FOR OTHER DISTRICTS WITH 100+ TRANSFERS

	TRANSFERS OUT				TRANSFERS IN				TOTAL DISTRICT ENROLLMENT			
	1993	1994	1995	1996	1993	1994	1995	1996	1993	1994	1995	1996
LOWELL	56	142	152	160	0	0	0	0	13988	14313	14693	14693
PITTSFLD	46	72	113	111	0	0	0	0	6531	6573	6854	6854
SALEM	24	56	104	80	0	0	0	0	4353	4570	4757	4757
WORCESTER	59	93	109	137	0	0	0	0	21476	21999	22568	22568
TRITON		112	219	220	19	15	103	124	2788	2892	3032	3032
AMESBURY	17	122	142	162	13	59	83	118	2575	2658	2709	2709
AYER	108	122	105	126	8	35	73	111	1777	1389	1389	1389
CLINTON	23	60	102	91	0	19	10	62	1758	1741	1807	1807
MILFORD	57	96	120	141	63	74	105	100	3821	3818	3828	3828

NET TRANSFERS AS % OF TOTAL ENROLLMENT					NET TRANSFER GAINS/LOSSES (NUMBER)			
	1993	1994	1995	1996	1993	1994	1995	1996
AMESBURY	1.0	-2.4	-2.2	-1.6	-56	-112	-152	-160
AYER	-5.6	-6.3	-2.3	-1.1	-46	-72	-113	-111
CLINTON	-1.3	-2.4	-3.4	-1.8	-24	-56	-104	-80
TRITON		-2.3	-3.8	-3.2	-59	-93	-109	-137
SALEM	-0.6	-1.2	-2.2	-1.7	N/A	-67	-116	-96
	-1.6	-2.9	-2.8	-1.9				
					26	-63	-59	-44
MILFORD	0.2	-0.6	-0.4	-1.1	-100	-87	-32	-15
PITTSFLD	-0.7	-1.1	-1.6	-1.6	-23	-41	-62	-32
LOWELL	-0.4	-1.0	-1.0	-1.1	6	-22	-15	-41
WORCESTER	0.3	0.4	0.5	0.6				
	-0.3	-0.8	-0.9	-1.1				

APPENDIX B

MASSACHUSETTS CHOICE STUDY QUESTIONNAIRES

Parent Questionnaire—Receiving

Fill in the following information from the postcard:

DISTRICT NAME_____ CODE_____

PARENT NAME_____ ID #_____

TELEPHONE_____ STUDENT Q.: YES   NO

PREFERRED TIME OF CALL: _____

	Date	Time	Comment/callback time
1st contact:	_____	_____	_____
2nd contact:	_____	_____	_____
3rd contact:	_____	_____	_____
4th contact:	_____	_____	_____
5th contact:	_____	_____	_____

FINAL DISPOSITION

1. COMPLETED INTERVIEW
2. PARTIAL INTERVIEW/TERMINATED
3. PARENT ILL/SICK/DECEASED
4. BUSY/NO ANSWER AFTER 5 CALLS
5. WRONG NUMBER [contact district for correct phone #]
6. LANGUAGE BARRIER
7. REFUSAL
8. OTHER (SPECIFY:_____)

Start of interview:

HELLO, MAY I SPEAK WITH [NAME ABOVE]? If/when that person is on the line, or if person asks who's calling: I'M CALLING FOR THE PIONEER INSTITUTE ABOUT THE SCHOOL CHOICE PROGRAM; YOU/[NAME ABOVE] HAD AGREED TO A SHORT INTERVIEW ABOUT THE PROGRAM. IS THIS A GOOD TIME?

If yes, or if [name above] not available but another parent will do the interview, proceed to Q. 1; if no, or if no parent at home, schedule a callback time.

1. COULD YOU TELL ME, FIRST, HOW MANY OF YOUR CHILDREN HAVE TRANSFERRED TO THE [DISTRICT NAME ABOVE] DISTRICT?

   ____ CHILDREN

2. COULD YOU TELL ME THEIR GRADE [S] AND NAME[S]? [if more than one: STARTING WITH THE OLDEST AND WORK TO THE YOUNGEST?]

	GRADE	NAME
A. OLDEST	____	_____
B. NEXT	____	_____
C. NEXT	____	_____
D. NEXT	____	_____
E. NEXT	____	_____

3. AND WHAT GRADE[S] WERE THEY WHEN THEY FIRST STARTED SCHOOL IN THIS DISTRICT?

   A. OLDEST   ____
   B. NEXT   ____
   C. NEXT   ____
   D. NEXT   ____
   E. NEXT   ____

4. DID [YOUR CHILD/ANY OF YOUR CHILDREN] ATTEND THIS DISTRICT AS A TUITION STUDENT BEFORE THE MASSACHUSETTS CHOICE POLICY WENT INTO EFFECT? Policy went into effect in the 1991-92 school year.

   1   YES   2   NO

5. WHAT IS THE NAME OF THE CITY OR TOWN IN WHICH YOU LIVE?

44	BROCKTON	600	ACTON BOXBOROUGH
97	FITCHBURG	18	AVON
107	GLOUCESTER	125	HARVARD
139	HOPKINTON	136	HOLLISTON
153	LEOMINSTER	162	LUNENBURG
163	LYNN	166	MANCHESTER
174	MAYNARD	168	MARBLEHEAD

Appendix B: Massachusetts Choice Study Questionnaires

```
    213    NORTHBRIDGE          304   UXBRIDGE
   _____   OTHER (SPECIFY:_____)
    code
```

6. IF THERE WAS NO SCHOOL CHOICE PROGRAM, WOULD YOUR CHILDREN ATTEND PUBLIC SCHOOLS IN [NAME FROM Q. 5] OR WOULD THEY ATTEND PRIVATE OR PAROCHIAL SCHOOLS?

    1   PUBLIC SCHOOLS
    2   PRIVATE SCHOOLS
    3   PAROCHIAL SCHOOLS
    4   NOT SURE

7. COULD YOU TELL ME HOW YOU FIRST HEARD ABOUT THE SCHOOL CHOICE PROGRAM? I HAVE A LIST OF SOURCES...(read list)

Code up to two answers:

    1   FROM NEWSPAPER ARTICLES OR ADS
    2   DIRECT MAILING FROM THE SCHOOL DISTRICT
    3   RADIO OR TV
    4   FRIENDS/RELATIVES
    5   OTHER (SPECIFY:_____)

8. COULD YOU TELL ME THE MAIN REASONS WHY YOU OR YOUR CHILDREN CHOSE TO ATTEND SCHOOL IN [DISTRICT NAME ABOVE]?

_____

_____

9. NOW I'M GOING TO READ A LIST OF REASONS SOME PARENTS GIVE FOR CHOOSING A PARTICULAR SCHOOL. COULD YOU TELL ME IF IT WAS A MAJOR REASON, A MINOR REASON, OR WAS NOT A REASON IN YOUR CHOICE OF [DISTRICT NAME ABOVE] SCHOOLS.

Codes for Q. 9:

1 MAJOR REASON   2 MINOR REASON   3 NOT A REASON

A. THE TEACHERS	1	2	3
B. THE ADMINISTRATORS	1	2	3
C. QUALITY OR DIVERSITY OF COURSES	1	2	3
D. HIGH ACADEMIC STANDARDS; MORE CHALLENGING	1	2	3
E. SMALLER SCHOOL	1	2	3
F. LARGER SCHOOL	1	2	3
G. GOOD ATHLETIC PROGRAM	1	2	3
H. OTHER EXTRACURICULAR ACTIVITIES	1	2	3
I. SAFETY	1	2	3
J. FACILITIES AND RESOURCES	1	2	3
L. CONVENIENCE	1	2	3
M. CHILD'S FRIENDS TRANSFERRED	1	2	3
N. A CHANGE IN ENVIRONMENT FOR YOUR CHILD	1	2	3

158 COMPETITION IN EDUCATION

10. HOW SATISFIED ARE YOU WITH THE [DISTRICT NAME] SCHOOLS AT THE PRESENT TIME? WOULD YOU SAY YOU WERE...

1. VERY SATISFIED
2. SOMEWHAT SATISFIED
3. SOMEWHAT DISSATISFIED, OR
4. VERY DISSATISFIED AT THE PRESENT TIME?
5. NOT SURE [DO NOT READ]

11. HOW SATISFIED DO YOU THINK YOUR [CHILD IS/CHILDREN ARE] WITH THE [DISTRICT NAME] SCHOOLS AT THE PRESENT TIME--WOULD YOU SAY...

A. If depends on child: older

1. VERY SATISFIED
2. SOMEWHAT SATISFIED
3. SOMEWHAT DISSATISFIED, OR
4. VERY DISSATISFIED
5. NOT SURE [DO NOT READ]

B. Younger

1. VERY SATISFIED
2. SOMEWHAT SATISFIED
3. SOMEWHAT DISSAT.
4. VERY DISSATISFIED
5. NOT SURE

12. WOULD YOU SAY YOUR CHILD[REN] WILL DEFINITELY STAY IN THE [DISTRICT NAME] SCHOOLS, PROBABLY STAY, PROBABLY NOT STAY, OR DEFINITELY NOT STAY IN THE [DISTRICT NAME] SCHOOLS?

1. DEFINITELY STAY
2. PROBABLY STAY
3. PROBABLY NOT STAY
4. DEFINITELY NOT STAY

13. HOW OFTEN DO YOU ATTEND PTA--PARENT TEACHER ASSOCIATION--MEETINGS AT THESE SCHOOLS? WOULD YOU SAY... [read list]

1. REGULARLY
2. OCCASIONALY
3. RARELY, OR
4. NEVER

14. WHAT ABOUT AT THE LAST SCHOOL[S] YOUR CHILD[REN] ATTENDED--HOW OFTEN DID YOU ATTEND PTA AT THOSE SCHOOLS?

1. REGULARLY
2. OCCASIONALY
3. RARELY, OR
4. NEVER

15. DO YOU HAVE AN OPINION ABOUT HOW THE CHOICE PROGRAM HAS AFFECTED SCHOOLS IN [DISTRICT NAME FROM Q. 5]? [if yes record]

_____

16. WHAT ABOUT THE [DISTRICT NAME ABOVE] SCHOOLS--DO YOU HAVE AN OPINION ABOUT HOW IT HAS AFFECTED THESE SCHOOLS? [if yes record]

_____

17. IN YOUR OPINION, IS THERE ANYTHING THE STATE COULD DO TO IMPROVE THE SCHOOL CHOICE PROGRAM?

    1   YES
    2   NO
    3   NOT SURE

18. If yes: WHAT WOULD THAT BE?

_____

19. OVERALL, COULD YOU TELL ME WHETHER YOU STRONGLY SUPPORT, SUPPORT SOMEWHAT, OPPOSE SOMEWHAT, OR STRONGLY OPPOSE THE CURRENT MASSACHUSETTS SCHOOL CHOICE PROGRAM?

    1   STRONGLY SUPPORT
    2   SUPPORT SOMEWHAT
    3   OPPOSE SOMEWHAT
    4   STRONGLY SUPPORT
    5   NOT SURE [DON'T READ]

NOW I HAVE JUST A FEW BACKGROUND QUESTIONS FOR STATISTICAL PURPOSES.

20. GENDER (Do not read)

    1   MALE
    2   FEMALE

21. WHAT IS YOUR AGE?

    _____   YEARS

22. WHAT IS THE LAST GRADE OF SCHOOL OR COLLEGE YOU COMPLETED?

    1   8TH GRADE OR LESS
    2   9 TO 11 GRADES (NO HIGH SCHOOL DIPLOMA)
    3   GRADUATED HIGH SCHOOL
    4   BUSINESS OR TECHNICAL SCHOOL
    5   1 TO 3 YEARS COLLEGE
    6   COLLEGE GRADUATE (BA OR EQUIVALENT)
    7   POST-BA SCHOOLING (MA, PHD, LAW, MEDICAL)

23. DO YOU OWN OR RENT YOUR HOME?

    1   OWN
    2   RENT
    3   OTHER (SPECIFY:_____)

24. ARE YOU A SINGLE PARENT OR GUARDIAN, OR DO BOTH PARENTS LIVE AT HOME?

    1   SINGLE PARENT/GUARDIAN
    2   BOTH PARENTS AT HOME

25. COULD YOU ESTIMATE YOUR TOTAL FAMILY INCOME FOR THIS PAST YEAR?

    (Read)   1 $75,000 AND OVER
              2   51,000 TO 74,000
              3   35,000 TO 50,000
              4   26,000 TO 34,000
              4   20,000 TO 25,000
              5   15,000 TO 19,000
              6   10,000 TO 14,000
              7   UNDER 10,000

26. WHAT IS YOUR RACE OR ETHNIC GROUP? (Read)

    1   WHITE
    2   BLACK OR AFRICAN AMERICAN
    3   HISPANIC
    4   AMERICAN INDIAN
    5   ASIAN
    6   OTHER (SPECIFY:_____)

THANK YOU VERY MUCH FOR YOUR HELP!

Appendix B: Massachusetts Choice Study Questionnaires

School Staff Questionnaire

NOTE: Q. 3-5 & 10-17 FOR SUPERINTENDENT ONLY

1. DISTRICT NAME_____ 2. DATE_____
3. TOTAL SEND_____ 4. TOTAL RECEIVE_____ 5. STATUS: REC SEND
6. STAFF NAME_____ 7. TIME_____
8. POSITION _____ 9. YRS _____
10. If not receiver: HAVE YOU EVER BEEN A RECEIVER? If yes: WHEN DID YOU VOTE TO STOP

    1 NO   2 YES   DATE: _____

IF RECEIVER, ASK Q. 11-16; IF NOT, GO TO Q. 17

11. WHEN DID COMMITTEE VOTE TO BECOME RECEIVER?

    _____DATE

12. DO YOU EXPECT TO REMAIN A RECEIVER FOR FORESEEABLE FUTURE?

    1 DEFINITELY YES   2 PROBABLY YES
    3 PROBABLY NOT   4 DEFINITELY NO
    5 NOT SURE   COMMENTS:_____

13. DO YOU EXPECT THE NUMBER OF CHOICE TRANSFERS TO....

    1 INCREASE   2 STAY SAME   3 DECREASE

14. If increase: WILL YOU ACCEPT AS MANY THAT WANT TO TRANSFER, OR WOULD YOU PLACE A LIMIT ON THE NUMBER? If limit: APPROXIMATELY HOW MANY?

    _____ LIMIT   (CODE 999 IF NO LIMIT)

15. DO YOU TAKE ANY SPECIFIC STEPS TO PUBLICIZE THE SCHOOL CHOICE POLICY? [THAT IS, TO HELP PEOPLE IN THE AREA BECOME AWARE OF YOUR SCHOOLS AND YOUR ACCEPTANCE OF TRANSFER STUDENTS?] If yes or ask what this means, say I WOULD LIKE TO READ A LIST OF POSSIBLES...

    1 YES   2 NO

Check as many that apply: (1=YES)

A. _____ DISTRIBUTE BROCHURES/FLIERS ABOUT DISTRICT SCHOOLS-INFORMAL
B. _____ MAIL BROCHURES/FLIERS TO VARIOUS COMMUNITY LISTS
C. _____ PAID NEWSPAPER ADVERTISEMENTS
D. _____ PRESS RELEASES OR NEWS STORIES
E. _____ TV/RADIO ADS
F. _____ ANNOUNCEMENTS AT SCHOOL/COMMUNITY MEETINGS
G. _____ OTHER
DESCRIBE: _____

16. WHAT IS THE TUITION AMOUNT YOU RECEIVE FOR CHOICE STUDENTS?

_____ $

17. WHAT ARE YOUR APPROXIMATE PER CAPITA OPERATING EXPENDITURES?

_____ $

TURN ON TAPE RECORDER FOR Q. 18-23

18. If former receiver: [If not superintendent, say I UNDERSTAND THAT YOU USED TO BE A RECEIVER.] WHAT WERE THE MAIN REASONS YOU VOTED TO STOP BEING A RECEIVING SCHOOL?

_____

19. If receiver: WHAT ARE YOUR IMPRESSIONS OF THE MAIN REASONS STUDENTS OR PARENTS CHOOSE TO TRANSFER TO THIS DISTRICT?

_____

20. If sender: WHAT ARE YOUR IMPRESSIONS OF THE MAIN REASONS STUDENTS OR PARENTS CHOOSE TO TRANSFER OUT OF THIS DISTRICT?

_____

21A. If receiver: HOW ARE THE CHOICE TUITION FUNDS USED IN THIS DISTRICT--DO THEY GO INTO THE GENERAL FUND, OR ARE THEY RESTRICTED TO SPECIFIC USES?

_____

21B. If sender: HAVE YOU APPLIED FOR REIMBURSEMENT FUNDS (GET DETAILS)

22. HAS THE CHOICE PROGRAM HAD SPECIFIC IMPACT ON POLICIES AND PROGRAMS OF YOUR DISTRICT? Senders: probe for changes to stop outflow

_____

_____

Appendix B: Massachusetts Choice Study Questionnaires

23. WHAT CHANGES, IF ANY, WOULD YOU LIKE TO SEE IN THE MASSACHUSETTS SCHOOL CHOICE LAW AND ASSOCIATED REGULATIONS?

_____

TURN TAPE RECORDER OFF

24. NOW, I WOULD LIKE TO ASK YOU SOME SPECIFIC QUESTIONS ABOUT PROGRAM IMPACT, TO MAKE SURE WE COVER ALL AREAS. I'M GOING TO READ A LIST OF WAYS THAT THE CHOICE PROGRAM MIGHT IMPACT A DISTRICT, AND I'D LIKE YOU TO TELL ME IF ANY OF THESE THINGS HAVE HAPPENED TO YOUR DISTRICT OR SCHOOLS. (First read and explain response categories)

		INCREASE/ ADDED	HELPED MAINTAIN	REDUCED	NO EFFECT	NOT SURE
A.	TEACHING STAFF	1	2	3	4	5
B.	SUPPORT STAFF/SERVICE	1	2	3	4	5
C.	COURSE OFFERINGS	1	2	3	4	5
D.	SUPPLIES/EQUIP.	1	2	3	4	5
E.	EXTRACURRICULAR ACT.	1	2	3	4	5
F.	CLASS SIZES	1	2	3	4	5
G.	RENOVATIONS/UPGRADE	1	2	3	4	5
H.	BUILDINGS	1	2	3	4	5
		OPENED		CLOSED		

25. I KNOW YOU HAVE PROBABLY ANSWERED THIS, BUT I WOULD LIKE TO GET AN OVERALL SUMMARY OPINION ABOUT THE MASSACHUSETTS INTERDISTRICT CHOICE LAW AND REGULATIONS. WOULD YOU SAY YOU GENERALLY

1. SUPPORT CURRENT POLICY AS IS
2. SUPPORT CURRENT POLICY BUT WOULD LIKE CHANGES
3. OPPOSE CURRENT POLICY BUT MIGHT SUPPORT WITH THE RIGHT CHANGES
4. OPPOSE INTERDISTRICT CHOICE REGARDLESS

TURN RECORDER ON

26. JUST ONE LAST QUESTION: I'D LIKE TO ASK YOU ABOUT IMPACTS THE CHOICE PROGRAM HAS ON TRANSFER STUDENTS, BASED ON YOUR EXPERIENCE.

FIRST, WHAT ABOUT POSITIVE EXPERIENCES? _____

_____

WHAT ABOUT NEGATIVE EXPERIENCES? _____

_____

27. DO POSITIVE EXPERIENCES OUTWEIGH NEGATIVE OR VICE-VERSA?

    1 MORE POSITIVE   2 MORE NEGATIVE   3 EQUAL

28. ASK ABOUT CHARTER SCHOOLS

Appendix B: Massachusetts Choice Study Questionnaires

Student Questionnaire

Instructions: For each question, circle the number next to your answer or fill in the blanks as requested.

1a. What is the name of the city or town in which you **live**?

_____
(Name of city or town)

1b. What is the name of the public school district that serves the city or town where you live, **if different**?

_____
(Name of public school district, if different)

2. What is your grade? _____ Grade

3. What grade did you first start attending schools in this district? _____ Grade

4. Which of the following best describes how you get to school?

 1 School bus
 2 Your own car
 3 Public bus/train
 4 Car pool/Friend drives
 5 Parents'/Sibling's car
 6 Other/Combination (specify:_____)

5. Approximately how long does it take for you to get to school? _____ minutes

6. If there was no school choice program, would you attend public schools in your district of residence or would you attend private schools?

 1 Public schools
 2 Private schools
 3 Not sure

7. Was the decision to attend this school mostly your decision, mostly your parents' decision, or a joint decision?

 1 Mostly your decision
 2 Mostly your parents' decision
 3 A joint decision

8. What are the **main** reasons why you or your parents chose this school?

_____

9. How satisfied are you with this school at the present time?

   1 Very satisfied
   2 Somewhat satisfied
   3 Somewhat dissatisfied
   4 Very dissatisfied
   5 Not sure

10. How satisfied do you think your **parents** are with this school at the present time?

    1 Very satisfied
    2 Somewhat satisfied
    3 Somewhat dissatisfied
    4 Very dissatisfied
    5 Not sure

11. The following is a list of reasons some people might give for choosing a particular school. Indicate if the reasons on this list were a major reason, a minor reason, or not a reason in your choice of this school.

    1 MAJOR REASON
    2 MINOR REASON
    3 NOT A REASON

    A. The teachers 1 2 3
    B. The administrators 1 2 3
    C. Quality or diversity of courses 1 2 3
    D. High academic standards; more challenging 1 2 3
    E. Smaller school 1 2 3
    F. Larger school 1 2 3
    G. The athletic program 1 2 3
    H. Other extracurricular activities 1 2 3
    I. Safety 1 2 3
    J. Facilities and Resources 1 2 3
    K. Convenience 1 2 3
    L. Siblings and/or friends also switched 1 2 3
    M. Other 1 2 3
       (specify: _____)

12. Do you plan to stay in this district until you graduate?

1 Definitely stay
2 Probably stay
3 Probably not stay
4 Definitely not stay

13. Could you tell me how you or your family first heard about the school choice program?

1 From newspaper articles or ads
2 Direct mailing from the school district
3 Radio or TV
4 Friends/relatives
5 Other (specify:_____)

14. Do you find this school academically harder, easier, or about the same as the last school you attended?

1 Harder   2 Easier   3 About the same

15. What is your current approximate grade average this year?

1 Mostly A's   (over 3.75)
5 Mostly C's   (1.75 to 2.25)
2 Mixed A's and B's   (3.25 to 3.75)
6 Mixed C's and D's   (1.25 to 1.75)
3 Mostly B's   (2.75 to 3.25)
7 Mostly D's or F's   (under 1.25)
4 Mixed B's and C's   (2.25 to 2.75)

16. What was your approximate grade average in the last year of your former school?

1 Mostly A's   (over 3.75)
5 Mostly C's   (1.75 to 2.25)
2 Mixed A's and B's   (3.25 to 3.75)
6 Mixed C's and D's   (1.25 to 1.75)
3 Mostly B's   (2.75 to 3.25)
7 Mostly D's or F's   (under 1.25)
4 Mixed B's and C's   (2.25 to 2.75)

If you are in 9th grade or higher, answer question 17; otherwise, skip to question 18:

17. What do you expect to do after you graduate from High School?

1 Attend a four-year college or university
2 Attend a two-year college
3 Enter the military
4 Find a full-time job
5 Other (specify: _____)

18. In your opinion, is there anything that the State could do to improve the school choice program?

   1 Yes   2 No   3 Not sure

19. If yes, what would it be? _____

_____

20. What is your gender?   1 Male   2 Female

21. What is your age? _____

22. Does your family rent or own your home?

   1 Own
   2 Rent
   3 Other (specify:_____)
   4 Not sure

23. Do both your parents live at home?

   1 Both parents at home (include stepparents)
   2 Mother or stepmother only
   3 Father or stepfather only
   4 Other family (grandparents, foster home, etc.)

24. What is your race or ethnic group?

   1 White
   2 Black or African American
   3 Hispanic
   4 American Indian
   5 Asian
   6 Other (specify:_____)

25. What has been the single most positive experience you have had at this school?

_____

_____

26. What has been the single most negative experience you have had at this school?

_____

_____

INDEX

"A Critique of the Witte Evaluation of Milwaukee's School Choice Program, 22
"Robin Hood" effect, 68
academic outcomes/academic achievement, 5, 24, 27, 113, 121
Bachelor's degree (as measure), 51, 52, 53, 155, 158, 159, 161, 163, 164
Carnegie Foundation Report, 18, 19, 22, 27
case study districts, xi, 9, 40, 41, 43, 48, 51, 55, 74, 101, 147
    Change, 80, 82, 83, 93, 97, 101, 102, 105, 107, 109, 116
    No Change, 80, 90, 101, 102, 105, 107, 109
    No Effect, 80, 82, 83, 84, 86, 93, 94, 96, 97, 98, 99, 100, 101, 102, 105, 107, 108, 109, 116, 128, 130, 131, 134
Chapter 70, 34
charter schools, viii, 5, 7, 13, 28, 29, 30, 33, 38, 39, 48, 49, 58, 60, 75, 136, 137, 139, 146
Chase, Arthur E. (state senator), 36
Chubb, John E., ix, 14, 15, 16, 31
citizen survey, 45, 137, 146
Claibourn, Michele, 22
class sizes, 81, 86, 91, 92
Colopy, Kelly, 26, 28
Cookson, Peter W., 14
Des Moines, 19
desegregation, 3, 5, 14, 18, 19, 139, 211
district staff interviews, xi, 81, 82, 83, 84, 87, 101, 109, 144
dropout rates, 27, 40, 54
Edelman, Nancy J., 26
Education Reform Act of 1993, 2, 35, 104
Educational CHOICE Charitable Trust, 24, 25, 137, 156, 157, 159, 161, 162, 163, 164
Elam, Stanley M., 19
Ellman, Tara, 27
Elmore, Richard, 17
Exit, Voice, and Loyalty, 15
financial impacts of choice, 4, 5, 29, 68, 74, 82
Finn, Chester E., Jr., x, 30
Fossey, Richard, 27, 47, 48
foundation program/foundation aid, 7, 10, 48, 71, 82, 88, 105, 106, 107, 109, 144, 148
Fuller, Bruce, xi, 17
Funkhouser, Janie E., 28
Gallup poll, 19
Golden Rule Insurance Company, 24
grade level trends, 37, 97
Hammar, Rosalind, 26
High School Graduation Incentive Program, 25, 26
Hirschman, Albert O., 15
income, 2, 3, 6, 9, 10, 19, 20, 21, 23, 24, 27, 30, 31, 34, 35, 47, 49, 54, 55, 69, 100, 106, 117, 120, 134, 140, 146, 147, 148
interdistrict choice, ix, x, 1, 2, 4, 5, 6, 7, 8, 9, 10, 17, 18, 19, 27, 29, 33, 36, 37, 38, 39, 48, 49, 50, 55, 58, 60, 61, 74, 76, 77, 78, 105, 111, 112, 119, 123, 130, 134, 136, 137, 139, 143, 145, 146, 147, 148, 149
    advertising, 10, 79, 148
    definition, 13
    enrollment, ix, 1, 2, 4, 5, 6, 7, 18, 19, 20, 21, 25, 26, 30, 32, 34, 35, 36, 38, 39, 40, 41, 43, 47, 49, 50, 51, 52, 58, 60, 61, 62, 65, 67, 68, 69, 71, 74, 75, 76, 81, 82, 85, 92, 93, 94, 97, 98, 99, 100, 101, 102, 103, 107, 108, 116, 128, 130, 134,

141, 142, 143, 144, 145, 149
law, 1, 3, 5, 33, 35, 36, 37, 43, 48, 62, 68, 78, 81, 82, 87, 91, 93, 96, 97, 103, 111, 112, 113, 119, 120, 121, 127, 130, 131, 132, 143, 147
parental satisfaction, 23
participation, 2, 8, 9, 10, 18, 19, 23, 26, 36, 123, 137, 139, 146, 148, 149
trends, 36, 43, 81, 82, 93, 94, 96, 97, 98, 99, 100, 101, 102, 106
intradistrict choice, 13, 14, 30
Iowa, 19, 20, 149
Kilgore, Sally J., 24, 27
mandatory participation, 8, 10, 14, 20, 25, 120, 121, 125, 146, 148
market competition thesis, 1, 4, 5, 7, 31, 41, 78, 79, 80, 93, 109, 111, 141, 143
Massachusetts, ix, x, 1, 2, 3, 4, 5, 6, 7, 9, 11, 14, 15, 18, 19, 21, 25, 27, 29, 30, 32, 33, 34, 36, 37, 39, 40, 41, 43, 45, 47, 48, 50, 58, 60, 74, 75, 78, 93, 102, 104, 110, 111, 112, 113, 119, 120, 126, 134, 135, 136, 142, 143, 146, 149, 155
Massachusetts Charter School Initiative, 1996 Report, 39
Massachusetts Department of Education, 30, 39, 40, 48, 126
Meier, Kenneth J., 17
METCO, 5, 7, 8, 33, 37, 38, 39, 48, 49, 58, 60, 75, 137, 139, 145, 146
Milawukee Parental Choice Program, 21, 23
Milwaukee Parental Choice Program, 21, 22
Minnesota, 19, 20, 25, 26, 27, 28, 29, 149
Minnesota's Public School Choice Options, 26
Moe, Terry M., ix, 14, 15, 16, 31

Nathan, Joe, xi, 26
Nebraska, 19, 20
Noyes, Chad, 22, 23
Open Enrollment Option (Minnesota), 25, 26, 28
Orfield, Gary, 17
Peterson, Paul E., xi, 22, 23, 24
Politics, Markets, and America's Schools, 14
Postsecondary Enrollment Option (Minnesota), 25
Pritchard, Kim M., 22
racial representation, 5, 7, 8, 48, 61, 75, 76, 145, 146, 147
reading scores/reading achievement, 56
Rose, Lowell C., 19
Rubenstein, Michael C., 26
School Choice in Massachusetts Good Intentions Gone Awry, 36
Smith, Kevin B., 17
state comparisons, 18, 50, 56, 135
survey findings, 6, 43, 82, 93, 101, 103, 107, 111, 142, 143, 147
Tarr, Hope C., 26
Thorn, Christopher A., 22
transportation assistance, 8, 9, 10, 16, 19, 35, 133, 134, 140, 146, 147
tuition payments/tuition reimbursement, 3, 4, 9, 10, 11, 13, 21, 33, 34, 35, 36, 38, 40, 43, 48, 49, 50, 55, 69, 71, 74, 78, 80, 81, 82, 87, 93, 94, 97, 98, 99, 100, 101, 103, 105, 106, 107, 119, 132, 133, 144, 148, 149
vocational districts, 67
voucher plans/voucher systems, viii, 13, 18, 21, 22, 24, 77, 136, 137, 138
Weinschrott, David J., 24, 27
Who Chooses? Who Loses? Culture, Institutions, and the Unequal Effects of School Choice, 17
Witte, John F., 21, 22, 24
Ysseldyke, James, 26

ABOUT THE AUTHORS

David J. Armor received his Ph. D. in Sociology from Harvard University in 1966. He has held appointments at Harvard, Rutgers University, and the University of California at Los Angeles. He is currently a research professor in the Institute of Public Policy at George Mason University, Fairfax, Virginia. He has served as Principal Deputy Assistant Secretary of Defense, has appeared as an expert witness in school desegregation court cases, and has written extensively on education, health, and military issues for publications that include *The Public Interest, The American Sociological Review* and *Policy Review*. His book *Forced Justice: School Desegregation and the Law* was published by Oxford University Press in 1995.

Brett M. Peiser holds a B.A. from Brown University and a Master's in Public Policy from the John F. Kennedy School of Government at Harvard University. He spent several years teaching high school in New York City.

PIONEER PAPER SERIES

Pioneer Paper No. 12, *Competition in Education: A Case Study of Interdistrict Choice* by David J. Armor and Brett M. Peiser, 1997.

Pioneer Paper No. 11, *Toward a Safer Workplace: Reform and Deregulation of Workers' Compensation* by James R. Chelius and Edward Moscovitch, 1996.

Pioneer Paper No. 10, *Bilingual Education in Massachusetts: The Emperor Has No Clothes* by Christine H. Rossell and Keith Baker, 1996.

Pioneer Paper No. 9, *Agenda For Leadership* edited by James A. Peyser, 1994.

Pioneer Paper No. 8, *Special Education: Good Intentions Gone Awry* by Edward Moscovitch, 1994.

Pioneer Paper No. 7, *Reinventing the Schools: A Radical Plan for Boston* by Steven F. Wilson, 1992.

Pioneer Paper No. 6, *By Choice or By Chance? Tracking Values in Massachusetts' Public Spending* by Herman B. Leonard, 1992.

Pioneer Paper No. 5, *School Choice in Massachusetts* by Abigail Thernstrom, 1991.

Pioneer Paper No. 4, *Mental Retardation Programs: How Does Massachusetts Compare?* by Edward Moscovitch, 1990.

Pioneer Paper No. 3, *Work and Welfare in Massachusetts: An Evaluation of the ET Program* by June O'Neill, 1990.

Pioneer Paper No. 2, *The Cost of Regulated Pricing: A Critical Analysis of Auto Insurance Premium Rate Setting in Massachusetts* by Simon Rottenberg, 1989.

Pioneer Paper No. 1, *The Massachusetts Health Plan: The Right Prescription* by Attiat Ott and Wayne B. Gray, 1988.

FORTHCOMING FROM PIONEER

The Effects of Government on Private Providers of Social Services, by Joe Loconte, Spring 1997.

Economic Development Policies, by Edwin S. Mills, summer 1997.

PROPERTY OF
PUBLIC INTEREST
INSTITUTE